STORIES OF WALES

The mermaid turned her lovely face towards Pergrin

STORIES OF WALES.

Told for Children by

Elisabeth Sheppard-Jones

with illustrations by Paul Hogarth

JOHN JONES CARDIFF LTD.

This book was originally published by Thomas Nelson
& Sons Ltd under the title Welsh Legendary Tales.

This edition © JOHN JONES CARDIFF LTD.
first published March 1976
reprinted October 1977

Text © ELISABETH SHEPPARD-JONES 1959

ISBN 0 902375 41 5

JOHN JONES CARDIFF LTD
41 Lochaber Street
Cardiff CF2 3LS

Academy Press Limited Edition 1978
Printed and bound in the United States of America

Academy Press Limited
360 N. Michigan Avenue, Chicago IL 60601

This book is dedicated to
THE CHILDREN OF PENARTH

Contents 🌀

Illustrations ᘛᘚ

Colour plates

ᘛᘚ   ᘛᘚ   ᘛᘚ

The Fisherman and the Mermaid ✌

PERGRIN was a fisherman who lived in a fishing-village in Pembrokeshire, and every day, no matter how bad the weather, he went out to sea in his boat to catch the fish by which he made his living.

Pergrin loved the sea ; he loved it when it was still and quiet and blue, because then it was his friend and treated him with care and gentleness, letting his boat slide smoothly across the mirror of its waters, and letting him fill his nets peacefully with the silver fish that swam in its depths. But he loved it, too, when it was wild and stormy and black because then, although it was his enemy trying to swamp his boat and drag him down to the bottom of the ocean, it was an exciting enemy to fight. There were times, of course, when Pergrin was not at all sure he was going to beat the sea in its fighting mood, for many of the fishermen in his village had been drowned. A fisherman's job is often a dangerous one.

One day, when the sea was in its friendly mood, Pergrin rowed well out from the shore before throwing his nets over the side of the boat. Then he sat and waited for the nets to fill with fish. Soon he began to haul in his nets. Recently Pergrin had not been getting big catches so now he was pleased when he felt the heavy weight in his hands.

' My goodness, I've a big catch here,' he said to himself, straining to pull the net over the edge of the boat.

Heaving and struggling, he managed to get in the net and there, lying on the floor of the boat in the midst of a heap of tiny slippery fish, was the reason for the weight. Staring up at Pergrin was a beautiful mermaid, the first he had ever seen, although he had often heard about them and occasionally had actually heard them singing when he returned to shore at night. Her green eyes were wide with fright, her long green hair dripped like sea-weed to her waist, and her long fish's tail glittered green and blue in the morning sun.

'Well!' exclaimed Pergrin.

Then, 'Well, well!' and then, 'Well,' again.

He wasn't sure what he should do. Surely a mermaid must be a very valuable catch; there was no knowing how much he would get for her in the fish market. Certainly no fisherman he had ever known had caught a mermaid in his net. On the other hand, she was big to handle and he could hardly treat her as he would any ordinary fish. She wasn't human, it was true, but then neither was she wholly fish.

While he was worrying about his problem, the mermaid suddenly spoke, and her voice was like the music you can hear when you put a shell to your ear, like the waves on the shore, like little rock pools on the beach, like sea anemones, like coral reefs, like caverns under the water. Her voice was the voice of the sea, yet her words were the words of Pergrin's own language, spoken carefully and slowly as if she were not used to them.

'Please, kind sir,' she said, her green eyes filling with sea-green salt tears, 'please, kind sir, put me back into the water. I want to go home. Please, please, kind sir!'

Imploringly she held out her little white hands whose fingers were tipped with pale shell-pink nails.

THE FISHERMAN AND THE MERMAID

Pergrin had a kind heart, and was sorry to see how distressed this lovely mermaid was. It would have been fun to take her home ; it would have been pleasant to have the admiring praise of the other villagers ; it would have been fine to have the money she would fetch if he could sell her, for he was a poor man and lately had earned even less money than usual. He hesitated.

' If you will let me go, kind sir,' said the mermaid, trying to smile at him through her tears, ' you will not be sorry, for should you ever be in danger at sea, I would help you. I would cry out to you three times to warn you to return to land. Please, kind sir, put me back into the water.'

She need not have pleaded with him so earnestly for Pergrin had already made up his mind.

' Of course I'll put you back,' he said. ' I am only sorry that I have distressed you.'

He helped her out of the net—a difficult business because she slithered about so—then he helped her over the side of the boat. She dived into the sea, sending up a crystal spray of water with a flip of her green and blue tail. Then she turned her lovely face towards Pergrin as he began to take up the oars to row for the shore.

' Thank you, kind sir,' she sang out in her voice of the sea, ' and don't forget, I shall call out three times if ever you are in danger, and you must return to land immediately when I do so.'

Pergrin waved a cheery hand at her. He was sad to have lost her but glad that he had done as she had asked, and that she was now happily on her way home at the bottom of the sea just as he was on his way home to firm, safe land.

Some months later, when Pergrin had almost forgotten about his mermaid, he was once again at sea in his fishing boat, and once again the sea was in a friendly mood, or so it seemed to him, for the sun shone and the waters were calm. He sat in his boat, dreaming about nothing very much in particular, when he thought he heard a distant cry of ' Pergrin ! Pergrin ! ' He looked around him but could see no other boats near by. He told himself he must have imagined it, but then he heard the call again, a little nearer this time.

' Pergrin ! Pergrin ! '

There could be no mistake, someone was calling him. And where had he heard that sweet voice before ? Suddenly he remembered. It was the voice of the mermaid. She had said she would call him three times if he were in danger. Surely he couldn't be in danger now ; the weather was perfect and the sea calm, but she had only called out twice so perhaps this was not the promised warning after all.

' Pergrin ! Pergrin ! ' the voice called out again.

This time it was much nearer, although he could see no sign of the mermaid even now.

' Ship your nets, Pergrin, and return to shore. Ship your nets and return to shore.'

The mermaid had called out three times, and the last time there could be no doubt about her warning. Pergrin looked up at the clear blue sky ; he looked down at the clear blue sea. Could the mermaid be teasing him ? There was no sign of storm, and he would look a fool returning to shore in the middle of a fine morning like this. What could he say when he was asked why he had returned ? ' The mermaid told me to return ' ? Why, he would be laughed at if he said such a thing. And yet the mermaid had appeared grateful to him, she had promised to warn him if danger approached, and she had seemed sincere. He remembered clearly her pale serious face with the great green eyes.

4

THE FISHERMAN AND THE MERMAID

Slowly he hauled in his nets and set the boat toward the shore. Slowly he rowed back, still not sure he was doing the right thing. But when he was half-way there he noticed the sky had darkened, that great black clouds had rolled over the blue sky and the golden sun, turning the bright morning into darkest night. It looked as if the mermaid might have been right, and Pergrin now quickened his rowing. It was hard to move the boat through the water for the sea had in a second become a heaving, angry mass of enormous waves.

Pergrin struggled on. This was as bad as any storm at sea he had ever experienced, and he was afraid it would be worse yet. It seemed to him hours before he reached the shore and, as he dragged his boat to safety, he looked out to that part of the sea where he had been fishing when the mermaid called him. The lightning flashed, the wind roared and the waves were higher than the tallest mountains of Wales. Pergrin's fishing boat could never have battled against such overwhelming odds but would have been sucked down, Pergrin with it, to a watery grave. How thankful he was that he had heeded the mermaid's warning!

' Thank you, little mermaid,' he murmured, ' thank you for saving my life.'

Above the crash and thunder of the raging storm, he thought he heard a sweet sea voice cry out, ' Goodbye, Pergrin, goodbye, goodbye ! '

The Fairies' Revenge ୬✦

THERE was once a farmer of Pantannas in Glamorgan, and
some of the fields on his land were favourite haunts of the
fairies. They often went there to dance in the green grass, to
sing and make music and, of course, they couldn't do any of
these things without making a great deal of noise. The farmer
must have been a bad-tempered man because he began to hate
the fairies, and considered them such a nuisance that he visited
an old witch in the district to ask her advice about them.

'These wretched fairies are a great trial to me,' he told the
old woman, 'and I should like to know how I can get rid of
them.'

'Well, well,' grunted the old witch, 'and what 'll you give me
if I tell you, eh? Can I have an evening's milk from your farm?'

The farmer agreed to this; it was common practice in that
county to give the whole of one milking to men taken on as
extra labour at harvest time, and the witch's request was not an
unusual one.

'To rid yourself of the fairies all you have to do is plough
up the fields where they meet,' advised the old woman. 'Fairies
like the green grass and when they find it gone, they will be
annoyed, and never return to bother you again.'

Pleased with the advice he had received, the farmer of
Pantannas returned to his farm and did as he had been told.
After the fields had been ploughed no fairy was heard or seen

in them, and complete silence reigned where once had been heard the music, chattering and laughter that had so annoyed the farmer. He sowed the land with wheat, and in the spring the fields were thick with the young green shoots.

One evening when the farmer was returning home from his fields he saw on the path in front of him a tiny man, dressed in green breeches and a scarlet coat. The little man approached the farmer and, boldly drawing a tiny sword, he pointed it at him, saying in a high-pitched squeaky voice :

' Vengeance comes, and it approaches fast.'

The farmer began to laugh at what he thought was a silly little man pretending to be very bold, but he didn't laugh for long ; something about the stern looks of the little fellow frightened him. However he said nothing, and walked quickly on his way.

A few nights later as the farmer and his family were preparing for bed, they were alarmed by a loud noise. Following the noise, they heard a voice cry out :

' Vengeance comes ! '

Nothing more happened until a few months later when the golden corn in the fairy fields was reaped and stacked, ready to be carried into the barn next day. But that night all the wonderful harvest was burnt in the fields, and no ear or straw of it was left. This was obviously the work of the fairies, and the farmer was filled with regret that he had behaved so badly towards them ; better to suffer the noise of the little folk on his land than have them vent hatred and vengeance on him. As he gazed sorrowfully at his ruined crop, he noticed that the little red-coated chap was once more standing on the path in front of him, pointing his sword towards him as before and saying :

' Vengeance but begins ! '

The farmer's ruddy face turned white as marble, and he called out after the retreating figure of the fairy.

'Please, come back, come back and listen to me, little man.'

At first the fairy refused, but again the farmer implored him. The little chap turned round, looked sulkily up at him, and demanded :

'Well, what do you want ?'

'I'm sorry for what has happened,' said the farmer, 'and I am quite willing to let the fields grow into grass again. As you fairy folk liked them so much, you will be very welcome there as often as you wish to come, but please, please, do me no more harm.'

'Our King has decreed that he will have revenge on you,' was the reply, 'and nothing can alter that.'

The farmer began to weep, and the tears rolled down his cheeks and on to the fairy until he was in some danger of drowning in them. Perhaps it was this that made the fairy relent a little ; at any rate he now said :

'I'll speak to my lord about the matter ; meet me here at sunset in three days' time, and I'll let you know what he says.'

The farmer promised to do so, and, a little comforted, went on his way. The time came for him to keep his appointment and there, in exactly the same place, he found the fairy and listened eagerly to what he had to say.

'I spoke to my lord who has seriously considered your offer. He cannot alter his first decree.'

The farmer's face crumpled when he heard this, but brightened at the fairy's next words.

'However, as you have promised to return the fields to grass, he has said that the fairy vengeance shall not fall on you or your children.'

THE FAIRIES' REVENGE

This calmed the farmer who immediately went off to make arrangements for the ploughed fields to be returned to grass. Soon the fairies returned, and once more their sweet music and singing could be heard at night, but their noise no longer disturbed the farmer. Indeed he was happy and relieved to hear it.

A hundred years went by, and the farmer's descendants lived peacefully on the Pantannas farm. True, every now and again a voice would be heard in the house crying, ' Vengeance will come ! ' ; but this had been happening for so long that no-one took very much notice of it.

One Christmas time, Rhydderch, son of the present farmer of Pantannas, invited to supper Gwerfyl, his bride-to-be, a girl from a nearby farm. The family and the girl were sitting round the fire, warm and content after a feast of roast goose, when they were suddenly frightened by the piercing shriek of a voice that seemed to come from somewhere outside the house.

' The time for revenge has come ! ' screamed the terrifying voice.

The company rose quickly and went outside. There in the cold clear night they huddled together, and listened in silence and fear. For a moment they heard nothing but the turbulent bubbling of water from the nearby river Taff ; then from a pool in the river that was called the Black Cauldron, the dread voice rose again :

' The time is come ! ' it cried.

No-one present knew what this meant, and they returned to the house and sat down again round the fire. No sooner were they settled than a little woman appeared, seemingly from nowhere, and stood on a table near the window.

9

One of those present, his nerves no doubt shattered by what had just happened, said :

' And what do you want here, you ugly little thing ? '

' Quiet, chatterer,' replied the little woman. ' I had come here to tell of what is going to happen to one of this family. But now I shall not waste my time on you.' And she disappeared ; whereupon the voice from the pool, which had been silent during the little woman's visit, began again :

' The time of vengeance is come ! The time of vengeance is come ! ' On and on it went, until all at the farm were shaking with terror.

' Come, Gwerfyl,' said Rhydderch, ' this has been an unhappy evening for you. I will take you home,' and together the lovers went off towards Pen Craig Daf where Gwerfyl lived. There Rhydderch kissed her, said goodnight, and set off on the return journey to Pantannas. But, alas, he never arrived.

Days, weeks and months went by, and Rhydderch's parents were beside themselves with grief. What had happened to their beloved son ? Where was he ? When would he return ? At last, in desperation, they visited a wise old man who lived in a cave in the hills.

' What can have happened to our son ? ' they asked. ' We have searched everywhere for him, and cannot find him.'

The wise man could not help them. He listened while they told of the strange things that had happened on the night of Rhydderch's disappearance and then, shaking his head, he said to them :

' I can offer you no comfort. From what I have heard, the disappearance of your son is the direct result of the curse the fairies laid on Pantannas many years ago. You will never see Rhydderch again. He has been kidnapped by the fairy folk and, although he may appear generations later, he will not do so in your lifetime.'

If his parents accepted this fact, Rhydderch's sweetheart did not. Gwerfyl waited hopefully for his return, and remained faithful to his memory. Every morning at dawn she went to the top of a small hill and, her eyes full of longing, gazed in every direction to see if there were any sign of her lover returning. At noon she would go to the top of the hill again, and at sunset too. The years went by ; her youthful beauty faded. Still Gwerfyl made her pilgrimage. Everyone else had forgotten Rhydderch but not Gwerfyl ; and, at last, old and blind, death put an end to her hopes. She was buried not far from Pantannas in the Chapel of the Fan.

Like smoke the years passed away, and like the shadows of the morning the generations came and went until there was no longer anyone alive who remembered Rhydderch, although the story of his disappearance was often discussed, and it was said that no fairies had been seen and no fairy music heard since that terrible day so long ago.

Now, to return to that day, and to Rhydderch. A few minutes after he had said goodnight to Gwerfyl he had been lured away by the fairies. In fact they had taken him to a cave where their King lived and there, as he thought, he spent only a few days, and quite pleasant days they were. However, he was anxious to return home and to see his sweetheart ; and this request, when made to the King of the Fairies, was readily granted.

It was a beautiful day when Rhydderch stepped out from the cave and made his way towards Pantannas. With a mixture of fear and wonder, he noticed on the way that where once had stood the Chapel of the Fan now was nothing but ruins. Where, he asked himself, had he been these last few days that everything on his return should seem so strange ? And indeed how long had he been away ? Had it really only been a few days ? He turned his steps towards Pen Craig Daf, the home of Gwerfyl. But there no-one knew of whom he was talking ; the name of Gwerfyl meant nothing to them. Noting Rhydderch's strange appearance and his wild manner, the present occupants of the house took him for a madman. He hastened then to Pantannas. He easily recognised his father's fields and the farmhouse, but the men working in the fields were strangers to him, as were those who were busy in the farmyard. They bade him good-day politely enough but no-one seemed to recognise him as the son of the house.

The door of the farmhouse was opened by a young girl he had never seen before, and inside the house was much altered. Rhydderch demanded to see the farmer and when he arrived from the fields, was faced, not by his own father, but by another complete stranger.

' What can I do for you ? ' asked the farmer.

Haltingly Rhydderch told him who he was and begged for an explanation as to why everything was so changed at Pantannas.

' You say your name is Rhydderch,' repeated the farmer in amazement. ' Well now, surely it is not possible ! I do remember my grandfather telling me how a youth of that name disappeared from this farm in strange circumstances hundreds of years ago.'

The farmer moved nearer to Rhydderch as if to examine him more closely for what he suspected seemed scarcely possible ; as he did so, he accidentally knocked him with the walking-stick he had in his hand. Instantly poor Rhydderch, so many hundreds of years old, crumbled into a mere handful of dust. Nothing more was ever seen or heard of him, and thus the revenge of the fairies was complete.

Gwarwyn-a-Throt ⚘

G WARWYN-A-THROT was a Welsh bogie, that is to say,
a mischievous elf, and his strange name, when translated,
means 'white-necked with a trot', so we can imagine he had a
long white neck and walked or jogged along, rather like a young
pony.

Long ago, on a farm in Monmouthshire, a merry, strong
young girl worked as a servant, and Gwarwyn-a-throt was her
friend. No-one knew where the girl came from, perhaps she
even came from fairyland, but when she arrived at the farm
the elf came with her. And very useful he proved. He helped
her in the house, washed, ironed, and spun wool. He asked
little reward in return for his work, just a bowl of sweet milk
and some white bread once a day. The girl, although she
knew he was there, never saw him; he did his work for her
at night while she was asleep. Every evening, before she went
to bed, she placed his bowl of milk and his bread at the foot
of the stairs, and every morning she found the bowl empty,
the bread gone and the work done.

The girl was grateful to Gwarwyn-a-throt but she was a girl
who liked a joke, and one evening, for fun, instead of filling his
bowl with milk she filled it with some of the dye that was used
for dyeing the wool. When the elf took a gulp from his bowl
that night he thought the trick far from funny. The dye tasted

horrid and, spluttering and choking, he danced around with fury at the bottom of the stairs.

The girl was soon to regret her joke. When she got up next morning she was suddenly seized by the neck, and the enraged elf proceeded to beat and kick her from one end of the house to the other. She screamed for help and, when some servant men ran to her aid, Gwarwyn-a-throt let go of her and ran off as fast as his spindly little legs would carry him.

Gwarwyn-a-throt came to the conclusion that he was not properly appreciated at this particular farm, so he moved to another one near by. Here the servant girl welcomed him gladly and fed him excellently, providing almost more bread and milk than he could eat. He worked well for her, and proved especially good at spinning and winding wool. As before, he never allowed the girl to see him and, as fairies often like to keep their names secret, neither did he tell her his name. In time she became curious, and one evening when she was alone in the kitchen, she said :

' Bogie, wherever you are, and I know you are somewhere here, come out from your corner and tell me your name. Do, there's a good bogie.'

' No,' replied Gwarwyn-a-throt, ' that I will not.'

As the weeks went on the girl became determined to find out his name, but every time she asked him she met with the same reply :

' No, that I will not.'

One afternoon, however, when everyone was out, she, too, decided to play a trick on him. He was spinning at the wheel ; she could not see him, of course, but she could see the wheel turning.

' I'm going out, bogie,' said the girl, ' and will not be back for some time. Carry on with your spinning,' and she left the room. The elf did not know that she had stayed just outside the door, and he began to sing at his work. This is what he sang in his high piping voice :

> *' If she knew, she'd laugh a lot*
> *To find my name's Gwarwyn-a-throt.'*

The maid threw open the door and cried out :
' Ha, ha, bogie, I know your name now, I know your name.'
' What is it, then ? ' he asked.
' Gwarwyn-a-throt, Gwarwyn-a-throt,' and the girl began to laugh.

She, too, was to regret her foolishness. There and then, the elf left the spinning-wheel and disappeared, never to return again.

This time he went to a farm where there worked a servant man called Moses. The elf had had enough of servant girls, and soon Moses and he became good friends. He worked for Moses as well as he had worked for the girls, and in return Moses gave him his required milk and bread. They lived together in harmony and only once did Gwarwyn-a-throt have a disagreement with Moses.

' Bogie, have you milked the cows this morning ? ' asked Moses one day.

' Yes, that I have indeed,' replied Gwarwyn-a-throt.

' From the noise they are making,' retorted Moses, ' I do not think that you have.'

' You are doubting my word ? ' screamed the elf.

' Yes, bogie,' admitted Moses, ' I am.'

Whereat Gwarwyn-a-throt set on him, pinching, scratching and biting him until he was black and blue. Later, when he found the churns full of milk, Moses apologised and, after that, the two remained the best of friends for many years.

Then troubled times came to England. Richard III, known as Crookback, was king but he was unpopular, and Henry, Earl of Richmond, gathered an army together to march against him. Now Henry was a Welshman and many of his countrymen joined his forces to fight the hated Richard ; among them was Moses. Gwarwyn-a-throt begged his friend not to go but Moses refused to take his advice.

' A King of England who is a Welshman is just what is needed, bogie,' he said, ' and I'm off to see we get him.'

At the battle of Bosworth, Henry won the day and gained the crown, but the good Moses lost his life.

When the news reached the farm, Gwarwyn-a-throt was inconsolable. He stopped working and sat all day, his head in his hands, moaning and crying. It was after he had lost his friend Moses that Gwarwyn-a-throt began to be troublesome, and almost impossible to live with. He annoyed the oxen when they ploughed, leading them astray ; he teased the hens, aggravated the cows and disturbed the seed the farmer had planted. In the house, he broke the china, spilt the milk, turned over the furniture and hid any small thing he found lying about. The farmer begged him to leave the farm, the farmer's wife implored him to leave the farmhouse, but Gwarwyn-a-throt continued with his naughty tricks.

The farmer became desperate and went to see a wise man who lived not far away, at Caerleon.

' Wise man,' said the farmer, ' the lives of my poor wife and myself are scarcely worth living. How can I rid myself of this wretched bogie ? '

' I bid you, bogie, to be transported to the banks of the Red Sea '

' I can help you,' replied the wise man, ' but it will have to be when the moon is full at the end of next week. I shall come to your house then.'

The wise man was as good as his word, and at next full moon he appeared at the farmhouse. He entered the kitchen and, sniffing the air, he soon managed to smell where the elf was seated, invisible, of course, to the human eye. Then the wise man closed in on him and, making a sudden grab, he managed to catch the elf by his very long nose.

' Ha, got you, bogie,' he exclaimed and, holding Gwarwyn-a-throt with one hand, he opened his book of magic and wisdom with the other, and read out a spell :

' I bid you, bogie, to be transported to the banks of the Red

Sea for fourteen generations and to be taken there by a strong, bold wind.'

No sooner had these words been uttered than there was a great rushing and howling of wind that made the whole house shake. This was followed by an even mightier whirlwind that whisked the elf from the wise man's grasp and carried him away. He was never seen again, and peace descended upon the farm.

The fourteen generations Gwarwyn-a-throt was to spend by the Red Sea are almost over and, who knows, he may turn up again in Wales any day now.

The Welshman and the Hazel Staff ✨

THERE was once a Welshman of Glamorgan who, never
having been out of Wales, decided he would spend a few
days in London. He found the capital of England a fine, interest-
ing place ; and he spent the time looking at ancient and historical
buildings, and wandering through the London streets that
were full of hustling, bustling people going about their daily
business.

This Welshman, whose name was Gwyn, had brought with
him from home a fine staff of hazel that helped him along the
way during his long walks. One day, as he was crossing over
London Bridge, an old man with a long grey beard caught him
by the arm, and said to him in a low voice :

' Excuse me, sir, but from where do you come ? '

Gwyn was annoyed to be stopped like this by a stranger.
He replied abruptly :

' I come from my own country, but I do not see why you
ask.'

His accent told the old man that Gwyn was a Welshman,
and now he said :

' All right, Taffy, do not be angry for I can give you information and advice that you may find most valuable. In your hand
you have a fine staff of hazel. Can you tell me where grew the
hazel tree from which this staff was made ? '

Gwyn wasn't sure that he wanted further conversation with

'Can you tell me where grew the hazel tree from which this staff was made?'

this strange old man, but something about his serious air made him answer the question.

'I cut the staff myself from a hazel tree that grows in a field near my home in Glamorgan,' he said.

'That hazel tree grows in a place under which are hidden great treasures of gold and silver, and if you can find the spot and will take me there, I can make you a rich man,' replied the old fellow.

Gwyn was a poor man; he had saved for a very long time before he could make even this one trip to London, and the thought of the treasure that might be his filled him with great happiness. He was afraid of this old man who knew these strange secrets but he soon overcame this fear, and together they returned to Wales, and Gwyn took him to the field where the hazel tree grew.

'We must dig here,' said the old man and, taking up the

spades they had brought with them, they began to dig at the root of the graceful old hazel tree. When they had pulled up the tree they found underneath it an enormous flat stone which, after much tugging and straining, they managed to move. Beyond the hole where the stone had been, Gwyn could see a dark tunnel leading to a large cave. He followed the old man into this, and when they were half-way down it they came to a bell.

' Be very careful not to touch the bell,' said the old man.

Gwyn edged past it carefully, for it was a big bell and there was little room between it and the wall of the tunnel. At last they came to the huge cave itself. To Gwyn's amazement it was full of sleeping men—soldiers. There they lay, fast asleep in a circle, their heads outward and their feet to the centre, with their swords and shields by their sides. One of these soldiers was a bigger man than the rest, and Gwyn recognised him as someone special because his sword and shield were covered with precious jewels, and he had on his head a crown of purest gold set with rubies, turquoises and diamonds. In the centre of the circle of warriors were two great heaps of coins, one of gold and one of silver ; and such was the sparkle of this treasure, the cave was filled with a wondrous light.

' Who are these sleeping men ? ' asked Gwyn in a whisper.

' King Arthur and his men,' answered the old man, ' sleeping here, century after century, until Wales has need of them. Now, Gwyn, help yourself to some of the treasure, but take only from one of the heaps, and only as much as you can carry.'

Gwyn carefully took from the pile of gold, filling his pockets with the coins, while the old man stood by, watching him.

' Do you want none of the treasure yourself ? ' asked Gwyn.

'No, I do not ; he who has wisdom has no need of gold,' said the old man. 'Are you ready to go now ?'

Gwyn nodded.

'Be careful then,' said the old man, 'not to touch the bell when we go out, for all, or some, or perhaps only one, of the soldiers will awake and ask if Wales has need of them. If, by chance, this does happen, be sure to reply "No, sleep thou on," and they will go back to sleep without harming you.'

It was as well that the old man had told this to Gwyn, for on his way back through the tunnel the weight of the gold he carried made him clumsy, and he accidentally touched the bell slightly. It tinkled, not loudly but clearly and sweetly. Instantly one of the warriors sleepily raised his head, and asked :

'Has Wales need of us ?'

'No,' replied Gwyn quickly, 'sleep thou on,' and the warrior immediately went back to sleep.

When they were out of the tunnel Gwyn and the old man put back the stone, and replanted the hazel tree where it had been before.

'Gwyn,' said the old man, 'before we part, I have some advice for you. There is no reason why, if you live carefully and are not too extravagant, the gold you have should not last you your lifetime but, if by evil chance, you need more gold, you may always return here for it. Never forget, however, about the bell, for if you touch it and give the wrong reply to the waking warriors, woe betide you.'

That was the last Gwyn ever saw of the wise old man. For some years he lived well and happily but soon he found he had spent too much of the gold, wasting it on things he did not need.

THE WELSHMAN AND THE HAZEL STAFF

' I must return for more gold,' said the greedy Gwyn, ' for soon I shall have none of this left.'

Off he went to the field where the hazel tree grew. As this time he had no-one to help him, it took all his strength to uproot the tree and to move the stone underneath it, but once he was in the cave the sight of the treasure renewed his vigour. He began to shovel the coins into a huge sack he had brought with him. He was tired when he had finished and, dragging the sack behind him, he slowly began to move down the tunnel, but the sack was so big he could scarcely avoid knocking the bell, and it was a heavy blow it received this time. Clang ! clang ! it rang out, very very loudly and still very clearly and sweetly. The noise was so great that nearly all the warriors instantly sprang to their feet.

' Has Wales need of us ? ' they shouted in chorus, their deep voices ringing through the cave.

Gwyn was terrified. There were many warriors, and the noise they made was very great. Also, he was tired and out of breath from the hard work of shovelling the gold into his sack. What was the answer to the warriors' question ? Try as he could, Gwyn was unable to remember what the old man had told him.

' No, no,' he said hurriedly, his voice trembling with terror, ' Wales has not need of you,' and as soon as he had said it he knew it was not the right answer.

The warriors set on him and began to beat him, then they took away his sack of gold, and threw him out of the cave. He managed to crawl on to the soft green grass near the hazel tree, and there he lay for some hours, too bruised to move. When evening came he limped home with great difficulty, his body aching and his heart heavy.

Many a day afterwards he spent looking for the entrance of the cave but, although he uprooted hazel trees by the dozen, he never found the stone that hid the entrance. Perhaps this was just as well for no man can be truly happy with too much gold that is too easily obtained.

Morgan and the Three Fairies ✒

SOME fairies like to know if humans are kind-hearted and, in order to find this out, they go, disguised in various ways, to cottages and farms. This is the story of the search of three fairies for kindness, and of the generosity with which they rewarded such a virtue when they found it.

One cold wintry night Morgan ap Rhys, who lived near the mountain called Cader Idris, was seated alone by a blazing log fire, puffing away at his old pipe, with a steaming hot drink on the hearth at his feet. Morgan was warm, happy and comfortable and, while he was congratulating himself on this state of affairs, there came a gentle rap on the door. Rat-tat-a-tat. Then, again, rat-tat-a-tat. Morgan was an hospitable man, ready to welcome out of the cold any travellers who might knock at his door.

' Come in,' he called, ' whoever you are.'

The door opened, and in walked three travellers ; at least to Morgan they looked like travellers. He was not to know that really they were three fairies in disguise. They greeted Morgan, and stepped towards the fire to warm their hands.

' Good sir,' said the tallest and thinnest of the three, ' may we beg a little food off you to put in this bag I have here ? We are poor men, and hungry ones too.'

Morgan instantly jumped to his feet.

' But, of course, of course,' he said, ' I should have offered it

25

before. Wait here a moment and I will get bread and cheese from the larder.'

He went out and soon returned with some crisp brown loaves his wife had baked that day, and a few hunks of cheese he had himself made from goat's milk.

'Here, take this,' he said, 'you are welcome to it, for as long as my name is Morgan I will never refuse those in want.'

The fairy travellers began to put the food in their bag.

'You are kind, Morgan ap Rhys,' said one of them, 'and we are grateful. Kindness shall be rewarded by kindness. We are not what we seem, and we have it in our power to grant you any wish you like. What shall it be?'

Morgan was very taken aback by these words, and it was a moment or two before he could collect his thoughts.

'A wish? Any wish? Well now, it's hard to say. I'm very fond of music. I've always wanted a harp. Yes, do you think I might perhaps have a harp?'

The three fairies whispered to each other, and then nodded.

'Yes, Morgan ap Rhys,' they said, 'you shall have a harp. We are going now, and you must close your eyes. When you hear the door shut behind us, you may open them.'

Morgan closed his eyes; he heard the door open softly, felt the bitter wind blow on his cheek for a second, heard the door close, and opened his eyes. There, in front of him, stood a beautiful harp, such a harp as Morgan had never expected even to see, let alone own. He touched it gently. He was not a very good harpist so it was with nervousness that he began to pluck the strings of this remarkable harp. For this was a remarkable harp, a fairy harp, and it could almost have played without Morgan's aid. Certainly the gay and melodious tune it struck up was none of Morgan's making.

MORGAN AND THE THREE FAIRIES

It was not long before Morgan's wife, who had been visiting friends, returned home, bringing with her a few of those same friends. His eyes sparkling, Morgan told them his exciting story and showed with pride the magic harp.

'Shall I play it to you?' he asked. 'Shall I show you how well I can play it?'

'Yes, yes indeed!' cried his wife and friends, 'go ahead, Morgan bach.'

So jolly and so merry was the tune Morgan played, they all felt forced to get to their feet, and round the room they danced and jigged, knocking over the chairs and tables, tripping over the mats, jostling into each other, bouncing, jumping, skipping. On played Morgan, the tune becoming quicker and quicker, and on danced the dancers, exhausted now but, while the music played, quite unable to stop.

'Please, Morgan,' panted his weary wife, 'stop your playing. I want to rest my feet.'

Morgan only laughed to see the strange effect his music had on his wife and friends, and still he played on. Wilder and faster went the music, higher and higher leapt the dancers. Now they all implored Morgan to stop and, when he saw how pale and tired they looked, Morgan did stop—but he went on laughing which made the company very angry as they didn't think the matter much of a joke.

As time went on Morgan and his fairy harp became well known in the district. Morgan loved the harp, and he loved the wonderful music it played when he touched its strings, but Morgan was the only person who did love it, because, whoever heard its music, could never refrain from dancing to it. As Morgan was always playing his harp, in his own house, in other

27

people's houses and out in the country, this proved to be very exhausting to its hearers, and it was not always very convenient. Old women with rheumatism, crouching by their fires, were forced to their aching feet ; farmers, tilling their fields, left their ploughs and capered in the furrows ; shepherds, tending their flocks, left the sheep to wander while they jigged on the hillside. Many people injured themselves, some slept for a week after dancing all night to Morgan's playing, and Morgan became very unpopular. However, he was enjoying himself greatly, and he refused to listen to the suggestions of his friends and neighbours that he play the harp less often, and out of hearing of anyone else but himself.

After a particularly long and exhilarating bout of playing one night, when his poor neighbours had suffered even more than usual, Morgan awoke in the morning and could not find his harp.

His neighbours, when questioned, said they knew nothing about its disappearance, but his wife remembered having seen three strangers, travellers perhaps, hovering around the house early in the morning when she went to milk the goats. Morgan had abused his fairy gift, and the fairies, deciding that they should show kindness to the people of the district of Cader Idris as well as to Morgan, took the harp away. Morgan, to his lasting sorrow and his neighbours' lasting joy, never saw it again.

John Gethin and the Candle ✌

THERE was once a wizard who was called the Man with an Iron Hand, and he lived near a mountain called Mynydd y Drum. It was rumoured in the district that under that mountain was hidden a great fairy treasure, and when this news reached the wizard he said to himself :

' Aha, with my magic and wisdom I could get hold of that treasure, but I should need help. Who, I wonder, would be brave enough to assist me in this adventure ? '

He began to search the neighbourhood for some plucky fellow to help him with his spells. He found John Gethin, and explained the matter to him.

' Will you help me now, John Gethin ? ' he asked.

' That I will,' said John.

' It will be a dangerous business,' warned the wizard. ' Are you brave enough ? '

' That I am,' said John.

That night the two of them went to the foot of Mynydd y Drum. There, taking up his magic wand, the wizard traced two rings on the grass so that they touched each other to form a figure eight. He stood in one of these circles himself and beckoned John towards him. John had been standing nervously in the background, wondering if he had been wise to come.

' Stand near me in this other circle,' said the wizard, ' and whatever happens, stay inside it.'

John stepped in and stood there waiting while the wizard busied himself with the huge book of spells he had brought with him. After he had murmured a few of the spells and made some weird signs in the air with his wand, there suddenly appeared a monstrous bull, and it bellowed so loudly that the very mountains seemed to shake and rumble with the noise.

John Gethin was tempted to turn and run ; but he stood his ground, and stared fearlessly into the fiery red eyes of the bull. Instantly the bull vanished. No sooner had he gone than there appeared a wheel of fire that hurled itself at John. This time he failed to stand his ground ; instinctively he swerved out of the ring to avoid being caught up by the flaming wheel. Thereupon the wheel turned into a triumphant devil who seized hold of John, and began to haul him away. The wizard grabbed John's other arm and tried to pull him back. Now there began a tug-of-war between the devil and the wizard with poor John in the place of a rope. It was soon apparent that the devil was the stronger of the two, so the wizard tried persuasion instead of force.

' Come, devil, let him go,' he pleaded ; ' let John Gethin go.'
The devil shook his head and pulled the harder.

' Look,' said the wizard, ' I have here a lighted candle that I brought with me that I might see to read my book of spells. Let Gethin stay at least while the piece of candle lasts.'

The devil agreed to this, and loosed his hold on his victim ; whereupon the cunning wizard blew out the candle, and the discomfited devil disappeared.

' Here, John, take this candle and keep it carefully, for you will last only as long as it does.' The wizard gave the candle to John, who put it in his pocket and went home.

John Gethin preserved the candle carefully, putting it away in a cool place but, although it was never lighted, a few days later he noticed that it appeared to be a little smaller. As time went on it grew smaller again, and John was so frightened by this that he took to his bed and, as the candle wasted away, so did he. They both came to an end at the same time and, as the candle completely vanished, so did the body of John Gethin. For the sake of appearances his relations had to put a lump of clay in his coffin !

That is the tale of poor brave John Gethin who was led astray by the promise of gold. The treasure probably still lies under Mynydd y Drum, and it seems best that it should stay there.

Robin Ddu 🦢

THERE was once another wizard, a very famous one, called Robin Ddu, which means Robin the Black—he was probably very dark-haired and dark-skinned. His powers were recognised throughout Wales, and many were the stories that were told of his wisdom and magic. One day a stranger who was doubtful about the wizard's power appeared in Robin's village.

'I don't believe he's a wizard at all,' the stranger told the villagers.

'Test him then,' they challenged, 'in any way you like.'

So the stranger caught a little robin red-breast and covered him over with a bowl. Then he sent for the wizard.

'They tell me you have great magical powers,' the stranger said.

'That is so,' the wizard replied.

'Well then, if you are so clever, tell me what I have under this bowl.'

Now, although Robin Ddu's wisdom was deep as the oceans, there were times when even he was unable to find the right answer, and this was one of them. He was not the type of man to pretend he knew something when he didn't so, without even looking at the bowl, he confessed that he was caught out.

'Robin is caught,' he said.

'You are quite right!' exclaimed the doubter as he lifted the bowl to let the little robin red-breast fly away.

Robin Ddu said nothing, but he smiled and told himself that luck was certainly with him that day.

The stranger went away full of awe and admiration for Robin Ddu. When he reached the next village he heard that the lady at the big house had lost a valuable ring, and he advised her to send for the wizard.

' If anyone can help you, he can,' said the stranger.

So the lady sent for Robin and tearfully told him what had happened.

' I have looked everywhere for my ring,' she said, ' and cannot find it, yet I am sure it was in my jewel box yesterday. My husband gave it to me, and when he returns from his visit to friends and finds I have lost it, he will never forgive me.'

' Do not worry, madam,' comforted Robin Ddu, ' I shall find the ring for you, rest assured. Go and lie down for an hour or so while I look around the house.'

Robin Ddu's wisdom sometimes enabled him to tell the thoughts of people merely by looking at their faces, and when he talked to the servants of the house he noticed that one of the maidservants blushed and twisted her fingers when he spoke to her. Dismissing the others, he asked her to stay behind for a minute or two. The girl did not look wicked, only very unhappy, and Robin spoke gently to her :

' Why did you steal your mistress's ring ? '

The girl began to sob.

' I didn't mean to do it, sir,' she cried, ' but the mistress left it on the bedroom table, and I picked it up before I knew what I was doing. I have no father, and my mother has a hard struggle to look after my little brothers and sisters. I suppose I thought if I sold the ring I could buy food and clothes for them. But it was wrong of me ; I'm an honest girl really, and I'm sorry for what

33

I did, but I do not know how to return the ring without being found out, and I could not bear the disgrace I should bring on myself and my family.'

' I can help both you and your mistress,' said Robin. ' You are sorry for your misdeed ; well then, we will say no more about it. Give me the ring, and I will think of a way of returning it so that suspicion falls on no-one.'

The grateful girl gave the ring to Robin and went back to her work, looking much happier.

Robin went to the kitchen and begged a piece of dough from the cook who was baking bread. Then he pushed the ring into the lump of dough and made his way into the garden, where the gaily coloured peacocks strutted up and down the terraces. There he threw down the dough, and noted the peacock who darted at it, and swallowed it up.

Then he sent a servant to ask the lady of the house to join him in the garden. When she arrived, he announced simply :

' I now know where your ring is, madam.'

' Where, oh where ? ' asked the lady excitedly.

' Order that peacock to be killed, and the ring will be found inside the bird.'

This was done and the ring, of course, was found. Robin Ddu's reputation for magic rose even higher, and only he and the maidservant knew that it was wisdom, not magic, that had triumphed that day.

There is another tale of Robin and a lost ring. This time it was a gentleman who had lost a ring and, hearing of Robin's earlier success, sent for the famous wizard.

' Will you use your magic to find my ring ? ' he asked.

' At any rate, I will use my wisdom,' replied Robin, and he

asked that a live cock and a cauldron that had recently been used on a fire be brought into the room. He turned the cauldron upside down on the table and placed the cock underneath it.

'Now send for the servants,' he said to the gentleman.

The servants filed in and Robin studied them closely, but this time the guilty person revealed nothing on his or her face.

Robin drew the heavy velvet curtains across the windows, shutting out the sunlight.

'Now,' he instructed, 'I want each of you servants to walk past the table, placing your thumb for a moment on the cauldron as you do so. The cock under the cauldron will crow as soon as the thief amongst you places his thumb there.'

Silently the servants filed past until the last one had passed the table, and yet the cock still had not crowed.

Silently Robin drew back the curtains and the sunlight streamed in again upon the startled faces of the servants. The gentleman broke the silence :

'The cock has not crowed so the thief cannot be here !'

'I think he is,' said Robin Ddu and, going over to the servants, he asked them all to show him their thumbs. There was only one thumb that did not have a black mark from the cauldron on it. Robin Ddu pointed to the owner of this clean thumb and cried out :

'There is your thief ! The only one who did not put his thumb on the cauldron lest the cock crow and reveal the truth. The others had nothing to hide.'

The Bride of Llyn y Fan Fach 〜●

TOWARDS the end of the twelfth century there lived on a farm in Llanddeusant, Carmarthenshire, a widow who had lost her husband in the wars. Her farmland was not big and her cattle had to be grazed on extra pasture on a nearby mountain. The widow had one son, and it was he who looked after these cattle. The animals always favoured the lush sweet grass that grew on the edge of a certain lake in the Black Mountains that was called Llyn y Fan Fach.

One day the widow's son was walking along the edge of the lake when, to his astonishment, there appeared on top of the water the loveliest lady he had ever seen. She was combing her long brown curly hair which flowed over her white and rounded shoulders. So amazed was the young man that he was unable to say a word, but he held out his hand towards her, and in his hand he had a piece of bread that his mother had given him for his dinner. The maiden glided nearer to him but refused the proffered bread, saying :

' Hard baked is thy bread ; see,
'Tis not so easy to catch me.'

Then she dived under the water and was lost to sight.

The young man had fallen deeply in love with her, and when he reached home he told his mother about the beautiful lady of the lake and how she had refused his over-baked bread.

' Don't worry, son,' said his mother, ' go to the lake again

She was combing her long brown curly hair

tomorrow and this time take some uncooked dough. Perhaps there was some spell connected with the hard-baked bread that made the lady refuse you.'

The next morning he set off for the mountain armed with some uncooked dough. Down to the edge of the lake he strode, and there he waited. The hours went by but no lake maiden appeared. Then he noticed that his cattle on the other side of the lake were in danger of wandering too near the water so he rushed round to see to them. And there, to his delight, he saw his lady-love, and she looked more beautiful than ever. He stretched out the uncooked dough to her, and this time he managed to tell her of his love and admiration, and he offered her his heart. She shook her head and murmured:

> ' *Unbaked is thy bread; see,*
> *I will not have thee.*'

But, as she disappeared beneath the water, she smiled sweetly at the young man and, though he felt unhappy, he was encouraged by this sign.

Hearing of his second failure, his mother made another suggestion.

' Don't worry, son,' she said, ' go to the lake again tomorrow and this time take some bread that is slightly baked ; perhaps that will please the lady of the lake.'

Early next morning he was off again to the lake in the mountain. All day he watched for the maiden. The cattle strayed, the sun shone, the rain fell, but the young man was aware of none of these things as he kept his eyes on the still waters of the lake. That evening, as the last rays of light began to ebb away and when he had all but given up hope of seeing the maiden again, she appeared. She approached the land, and he rushed into the water to meet her. She smiled at him, he took her hand and offered her the bread. This time she accepted it and, when he proposed marriage to her, she accepted him too.

' But,' she added, ' should you ever give me three causeless blows, I shall have to leave you for ever.'

Then the maiden loosed her hand from his, darted away from him and dived into the lake. As she did so, the young man noticed how beautiful were her feet and ankles and in what a strange fashion her sandals were tied. He was overcome with grief to see her go, especially as she had only just consented to be his wife, and he was on the point of casting himself into the deep water in despair when there arose from the lake a noble old man and his *two* beautiful daughters.

' Do not be disturbed,' said the old man to the young one. ' I understand you wish to marry one of my daughters ; you shall do this, provided you can tell me which of the two is the one you love.'

The bewildered young man looked from one lady of the lake

to the other, and then back again. They looked exactly the same, they had the same hair and eyes, and were the same shape and height. It was impossible to tell which was the one to whom, a few minutes ago, he had proposed marriage. He was about to give up the difficult task when one of the maidens thrust her foot forward. The young man instantly noticed it and also noticed the odd way in which her sandal was tied. Pointing to her, he said to the old man :

' That is the one I love.'

' You have chosen correctly,' said her father, ' Be a good and faithful husband to her. I will give her as a marriage dowry as many sheep, cattle, goats and horses as she can count without drawing in her breath. And remember, if you are unkind to her, or strike her three times without cause, she shall return to me, bringing with her all the stock.'

The young man agreed, and the maiden began to count the number of sheep she was to have. She counted by fives—one, two, three, four, five, and then, again, one, two, three, four, five quickly and as many times as possible until her breath was exhausted. Then she went on to count, in turn, the number of cattle, goats and horses. When she had finished the full number of each came out of the lake as her father called them, and they presented a fine and handsome sight indeed.

After they were married the young couple went to live at a farm called Esgair Llaethdy, near the village of Myddfai, and they lived happily there for many years, becoming the parents of three healthy sons.

No causeless blows had yet been struck, but one day husband and wife were invited to a christening. The wife was not very willing to go.

39

' It is too far for me to walk,' she complained, as they left the house.

' Well, go and fetch one of the horses that is grazing in the field over there,' said her husband.

' I will,' she replied, ' if you will go and fetch my gloves which I have left in the house.'

He went to the house and returned with the gloves. When he found his wife had not gone for the horse, he playfully tapped her on the shoulder with one of the gloves, saying, ' Not gone for the horse yet ! '

' Alas,' she cried, ' you have struck me the first blow without cause. Be more careful in the future.'

Some time later husband and wife went to a wedding. There were many guests and a great deal of merriment and rejoicing as there always is at weddings. There was feasting and dancing and a fiddler to play the music. In the middle of this jollity the wife suddenly burst into tears, and her sobs were piteous to hear. Her husband touched her on the shoulder and inquired :

' Why, my dear, what is the matter ? '

' Now people are entering into trouble,' she answered, ' and your troubles are likely to begin for, alas, you have just struck me the second blow without cause. There is only one blow left. We must both be very careful from now on.'

The lady of the lake loved her husband as dearly as he did her and had no wish to be separated from him or their clever children, and she prayed that nothing would happen to make her leave him. The happy years went by, and perhaps the husband became less careful. At any rate one day they were together at a funeral and, in the middle of the quiet mourning for the dead man, the wife seemed in the gayest of spirits, and she began to laugh out loud. Her husband, shocked at this outburst, touched her on the shoulder, saying :

' Hush ! hush ! don't laugh.'

' I laugh,' she said, ' because people when they die go out of trouble. But, alas, alas, you have struck me the third and last blow. Farewell, my beloved husband.'

She walked out of the house and back to the farm, where she began to call the sheep, cattle, goats and horses she had brought with her many years ago as her marriage dowry. They all obeyed her call ; even a little black calf that had been killed came alive and joined the others, and four oxen ploughing in a field left their work when they heard their mistress call :

> ' Come, you four grey oxen,
> Do not be so slow,
> Leave your hard work now,
> We must homeward go.'

Away they all went, following the lady of Llyn y Fan Fach across the mountain until they came to the lake from whence they had first appeared. There they disappeared beneath the water, leaving no trace, except for the furrow which was made by the plough that the oxen drew after them.

We know nothing of what later happened to the deserted husband of the lake lady, but her three sons often wandered by the lake in the hope that they might see again their lovely mother. One day they did. She appeared and spoke to the eldest son, whose name was Rhiwallon.

' You are to be of help and use to the world,' she said. ' I shall instruct you in the arts of medicine that you and your family after you may become great and skilful physicians. Whenever you need my advice, I will meet you.'

With these words she disappeared, but on several other occasions she met her sons and instructed them in medical lore, showing them where to find the best plants and herbs from which to brew healing medicines. Soon they became famous as physicians who were not only wise but also generous, and any sick people who needed their attention received it, regardless of whether they could pay or not. Rhiwallon's son and his sons and his son's sons inherited the knowledge and skill that he had obtained from his mother, the lady of Llyn y Fan Fach, and became famous throughout the country as the Physicians of Myddfai.

The Oxen and the Afanc ✌●

THE people of the Conway Valley were sorely distressed; for some time past their fertile land had suffered from a series of disastrous floods that drowned the livestock, ruined the crops and left the good earth unproductive. These floods, they knew, were not the result of natural happenings: they were the fault of the afanc. Now an afanc is a legendary Welsh water monster something like, say, the Loch Ness monster, and this afanc of the Conway Valley was an enormous beast who, every time he moved about in his lake, caused the waters to swell and break over the river banks. Many attempts had been made to kill him, but it seemed his hide was very tough and no spear, dart or arrow managed to pierce it.

A meeting was held in the market-place of one of the larger towns to decide what was to be done about this difficult problem.

'There's only one thing to do,' said a farmer. 'We'll have to drag the afanc out of the lake.'

'That's all very well,' said another man, 'but what do we do with him when we get him out?'

'We certainly can't let him roam about the countryside, doing further damage and frightening everyone into the bargain,' said a shepherd.

'But we could move him,' said the farmer, 'from his own lake to another one, higher up, near Snowdon, say, where he would be no trouble to anyone.'

43

Then a practical man spoke up from the crowd.

'May I ask just how it is proposed to move this afanc who, I understand, weighs a hundred times as much as the largest house in the district?'

At this question there was much murmuring among the crowd and a few vague suggestions, none of them very good. Then the farmer spoke again.

'We must use iron chains,' he said, 'and we must borrow the two mightiest oxen in the country, the long-horned oxen of Hu Gadarn, the twin calves of the Freckled Cow.'

The crowd acclaimed this suggestion with cheers and roars of approval.

'I'll make the strongest chains in the kingdom,' promised the blacksmith, and away he went to start his work at the forge.

It was a little later, when the iron chains had been forged and the famous oxen procured, that another problem arose. How were they to get the afanc out of this lake, bind him with chains and hitch these to the oxen? This was solved by the daughter of the farmer, who was a brave and lovely maiden.

'It is said that the afanc likes young girls,' she said, 'and I believe that I can persuade him to come out of the lake.'

The girl went down to the afanc's lake while her father and his friends stayed hidden a short distance away. Standing at the edge of the unruffled water, she softly called:

'Afanc, afanc, are you there?'

There was no sound, no movement. Again the girl called, louder this time, her voice rippling across the green water like music from a harp.

'Afanc, afanc, are you there?'

The waters began to heave and churn, huge waves broke at the edge of the lake so that the girl had to run back some yards

44

to avoid them, and out of the centre of the angry waters popped the huge head of the monster.

The girl was tempted to turn and race for home but, remembering how important it was to capture this troublesome afanc, she stood her ground and gazed fearlessly into the slimy green-black eyes of the monster.

' Afanc,' she said, ' why don't you come out of the lake and sit here with me ? I will sing to you.'

The afanc snorted, shooting sprays of water like fountains into the air.

' Come on, afanc dear, do come on out,' enticed the girl.

The afanc moved, and again the waters tossed and shook. Slowly the great body crawled its way out of the lake and towards the girl. He was so huge, she could see nothing above or on either side of him. The thick blackness of his leathery hide was such that night seemed suddenly to fall upon her as all light was blotted out. Still she did not move, and when the afanc ceased his heavy shuffling and lowered his bulk a few feet from her, she somehow managed to begin a quavering little song. She sang the sweetest and the most soothing lullaby she knew, one her mother used to sing to her when she was a baby in the cradle. Slowly the afanc's head sank to the ground, and soon the girl's song was drowned by an alarming noise that sounded like ten thousand claps of thunder. The afanc was asleep, and he was snoring !

The girl signalled to her father, and the people came from their hiding-place and very quietly set about binding the sleeping afanc with the iron chains.

They had only just finished when the afanc awoke and, realising the trick that had been played upon him, he bounded back into the lake with a roar of fury that threatened to crack the very mountains. Fortunately the chains were long and a few of the strongest men were able to grasp the ends and hitch them on to the mighty oxen they had brought with them. The oxen braced their muscles and began to pull. The afanc struggled and tugged in vain. Gradually he was pulled slowly out of his lake and on to the shore. Now the men, too, began to help with the pulling and, although it was the oxen who really did the job, one or two of the men began to boast.

' See,' said the farmer, ' how strong I am ; without me, the afanc could never have been dragged from the lake.'

' Nonsense,' retorted the shepherd, ' it is my great strength that has done the trick.'

' You are both wrong,' said the blacksmith, ' it is the strength I have in my arms, strength that I have gained during many years of wielding the hammer on the anvil, that is doing the job so well.'

Hearing this argument, the afanc, who well knew that without the oxen nobody could have moved him, spoke up, and this is what he said :

> ' Had it not been for the oxen's sake,
> The afanc had never left the lake.'

These words made the boastful men ashamed of themselves and their tongues grew quiet as the work of moving the afanc went on.

They were going to take him to a lake called Llyn Fynnan Las, and the journey there was long. Through the parish of Dolwyddelen the oxen heaved the afanc, then on through a pass that has since been called the Hilly Pass of the Oxen, and up through a mountain field. Here the oxen strained so hard to pull their heavy load the eye of one of them dropped out with the effort, and the field has since been called the Field of the Ox's Eye. The ox wept to lose his eye and his tears made a pool that has since been called the Pool of the Ox's Eye. On struggled the oxen until finally they reached Llyn Fynnon Las. Here they stopped and lay down, exhausted but full of pride at the magnificent task they had achieved. The chains on the afanc were loosed, and, with a roar, the monster leapt into the lake that was to be his new home.

The people of these parts had no objection to having the afanc there as the lake was already full of other unpleasant creatures, and was too far away from their good farming land for any damage to be done.

Einion and the Fair Family ✌•

ONCE on a time there was a young shepherd called Einion who was lost on the mountains he knew so well ; and this is the tale of his adventures.

It had been a fine and clear morning when he had set out with his sheep ; but, as the day wore on, a thick mountain mist began to fall and Einion decided to make his way home before it became worse. He took his crook firmly in one hand and began the homeward journey ; the mist was now so thick he could scarcely see a yard in front of him, and he wrapped his cloak closer round him to keep out the damp.

Einion thought he knew every rock and cranny of his beloved mountains, but it was not long before he realised that he had strayed off his familiar paths, and that he had lost his way. For hours he walked in all directions, trying to find some sign that would tell him where he was. At last he reached a low marshy spot where the reeds grew tall and thin, and the mud squelched beneath his feet ; and there, just in front of him, he saw a number of fairy rings. He stopped, aghast at the sight ; he had often heard of the terrible things that had happened to other shepherds who had strayed into the magic circles where the Fair Family danced.

Einion turned and ran quickly in the opposite direction but, however fast he ran and in whatever direction he ran, he always found himself back again near those fairy rings.

EINION AND THE FAIR FAMILY

After a long time spent running to and fro, Einion suddenly bumped into a funny little fat man, whose merry blue eyes peered at him in friendly fashion through the mist. Einion was not sure whether to be frightened at this odd meeting or relieved that he had met someone who could perhaps direct him on the right way.

' Hello, son,' said the stranger, ' what are you doing here ? '

' I am trying to find my way home, sir,' replied Einion miserably.

' Oh,' said the fat little man, ' follow me, and say not a word until I tell you.'

Einion obeyed until at last they came to an oval stone. The little man tapped this in the middle three times with his walking-stick, and then lifted it up. Underneath there appeared to be a narrow path with stairs, and from these stone steps there shone a bright greyish-blue light. Einion, dazzled by the light and still a little frightened, took a step back.

' Do not be afraid,' said the fat man, ' follow me, and no harm will come to you.'

On followed poor Einion, wondering fearfully what was going to happen to him. Down the path and down the steps they went until presently they came to a beautiful country where the land was fertile, the houses were splendid, and everything had the appearance of great magnificence. The water of the rivers sparkled in the sun, and the rivers themselves twisted like silver skeins through meadows green as emeralds, while the hills in the distance were soft as green velvet, their peaks lost in a lavender haze. By the time they had reached the mansion where the fat man lived, Einion was quite giddy with the sweet sights he had seen and the sweet singing he had heard as the brightly coloured birds carolled in the tall trees that surrounded

Presently they came to a beautiful country

the house. Inside the house, there was so much gold and silver that Einion's eyes were blinded for a second by the glitter of it.

Looking around him, Einion noticed many musical instruments, but he could see no-one who might play them ; and when his host invited him to sit at the dining-table, the dishes appeared and disappeared of themselves. Einion ate well for he was hungry after his long lonely hours on the mountainside, but he was puzzled. He could see no-one but his fat friend, yet he could hear people talking together around him.

As he had been instructed when he first met the strange little man, Einion had not said a word, but now the man said to him :

' You can talk as much as you like now.'

Einion tried to move his tongue to speak but he could no

more move it than if it had been a lump of ice. This quite frightened him but, at that moment, a dear old lady with rosy cheeks appeared and smiled at him. She was followed by her three daughters who were exceptionally beautiful. They, too, smiled at Einion.

' You are a handsome youth,' said one.

' What is your name ? ' asked the second.

' Where do you come from ? ' inquired the third.

But Einion was still unable to speak until one of the girls came up to him and gave him a kiss on his lips. That loosened his tongue, and he began to chatter away at his ease.

He was immensely happy in the company of this charming family, so happy in fact that he stayed with them for a year and a day without knowing that he had been more than one day in this magical country, where time did not seem to exist.

But soon he began to have a longing for home.

' Do you think I could go home ? ' he asked the fat man.

' Stay a little longer,' was the reply, ' and then you may go for a while.'

So Einion stayed, and whenever he talked of going away, Olwen, the maiden who had kissed him, looked sad and Einion himself could scarcely bear the thought of leaving her.

At last, after promising to return, Einion was permitted to go, and with him he was allowed to take gold, silver and precious gems in abundance. The journey was soon over, and Einion presented himself in the little village where he had once lived. No-one there knew who he was for they believed that the shepherd Einion had been killed by another shepherd who had taken himself off to America. Quite apart from that, it was difficult to recognise this gentleman, with his fine manners and clothes, as the shepherd lad who had been poor and ill-dressed.

Eventually Einion convinced the villagers that it truly was he, and he stayed among them for a short time.

It was on a Thursday night, at the time of a new moon, that he left as suddenly as he had done the first time. And as he had told no-one from whence he had come, neither did he tell anyone where he was going.

Great was the joy in the fairy country when Einion returned, and Olwen's delight was only equalled by his now that they were reunited. They planned to get married, and this they did with as little fuss as possible, for fuss and noise were much disliked by this family below the earth.

Again Einion wished to return to his own people but this time he wished his bride to accompany him. It took a long time to persuade the old man, but at last he agreed, and he gave them each a snow-white pony on which to make the journey.

Olwen and Einion rode down the main street of Einion's old home and, as the people came out to greet them, it was everyone's opinion that the shepherd's bride was the most beautiful woman they had ever seen.

The young couple settled down in the village where they received a warm welcome and much respect. Their wealth, which had come from the fairy country, enabled them to live well and to buy a huge estate. A son was born to them whom they called Taliessin.

The villagers sometimes questioned Einion about his wife.

' Where does she come from ? '

' Who are her father and mother ? '

' Why has she no relations to visit her ? '

But Einion never gave them satisfactory answers.

At last one of the villagers said to him :

' It is a strange situation, and it's my belief your wife comes from the Fair Family,' by which he meant Olwen was of fairy blood.

Einion's answer was a cunning one.

' Certainly,' he said, ' she comes from a very fair family, for she has two sisters who are as fair as she and, if you saw them together, you would admit that name to be a most fitting one.'

So, in the end, no–one was any the wiser although everyone continued to suspect that Olwen's real home was in the Land of Enchantment.

The Eagle and the Owl 🐦

THERE was once an old Eagle and because he was so very old, he was also very wise. Now this old Eagle was a widower and, his children and grandchildren and great-grandchildren having grown up and left him, he was very lonely.

'I should be much happier,' he told himself, 'if only I had a pleasant and wise companion to live with me. I think I shall have to marry again.'

He began to look round for a suitable bird to marry. He did not want a young and beautiful wife; he wanted someone old and wise like himself. The Nightingale, in spite of her lovely voice, did not interest him, he thought the Cuckoo silly and the Magpie flighty. The bird he thought might suit him was the one whose loud too-whit too-whoo rang through the woods at night. Yes, the Owl. He guessed that the Owl he had in mind was an old bird, but he wanted to make sure that she was as old as, or, if possible, older than, he was himself. He did not like to ask her what her age was—this might sound rude—and, being a woman, he wasn't sure she would tell the truth about it anyway. He decided the only way to find out about her was to ask one of his friends. He flew to his friend the Stag whom he found lying down by an old oak tree in the forest.

'Good morning, Mr Stag,' said the Eagle.

The Stag woke up with a start and yawned.

THE EAGLE AND THE OWL

' Oh, it's you, Mr Eagle, you surprised me. What can I do for you ? '

' Well,' explained the Eagle, ' I am thinking of marrying again, and I had in mind the Owl as my future wife, but I want to make sure she is truly old. As you yourself have been in the forest for as long as I can remember, I wondered if you could tell me how old the Owl is.'

The Stag shook his great head with its fine antlers.

' She is very old indeed,' he said, ' but exactly how old I cannot tell. I remember when this oak under which I am lying was but an acorn on the top of one of the biggest trees in this forest. It takes an oak three hundred years to grow to its full strength, it has another three hundred years in its prime, another three hundred it takes to die and decay into the earth which it is now on its way to doing, and I remember the Owl was old when I first saw the acorn. I tell you what, why don't you go and see the Salmon ? He is much older than I am and might well know something about the age of the Owl.'

The Eagle thanked the Stag for his help and went down to the river in search of the Salmon. He found the Salmon swimming lazily in the clear water of the river, the silver of its back gleaming brightly.

' Good morning, Mr Salmon,' said the Eagle ; ' I have been advised to come to you by my good friend Mr Stag.'

' Oh, yes,' said the Salmon, flipping its tail and sending little shoots of water into the air ; ' and what can I do for you ? '

The Eagle explained about the Owl and asked if the Salmon could tell him her exact age.

' I am very old,' said the Salmon ; ' as old in years as the number of scales and spots upon me, and yet the salmon who were old when I was but a babe could not themselves remember the Owl when she was young ; so, you see, she must indeed be very very old. But I have a friend, the Thrush, and he is older than I am ; go to him with your question and perhaps he will be able to help you.'

The Eagle thanked the Salmon, and flew away to find the Thrush. This took him some time but at last he found the speckled-breasted bird sitting on a small stone.

' Good morning, Mr Thrush,' said the Eagle ; ' I have been advised to come to you by my good friend Mr Salmon.'

' Oh, yes,' trilled the Thrush, dropping from his mouth a nice fat worm ; ' and what can I do for you ? '

After the Eagle had told him about the Owl, the Thrush was silent for a moment, then he said :

' You see this little stone here. Well, I am so old that I remember when this stone was too big for three hundred oxen to pull, but I have sharpened my beak on it every night before going to sleep, and I have brushed the point of my wings upon it every morning when I awoke. You can imagine how many hundreds of years it has taken for me to reduce the huge boulder to this pebble—and yet, old as I am, I never remember the Owl as anything but an ancient bird who looked as old as she does now when I was but a fledgling, new out of the nest. True, I am older than the Stag and older than the Salmon, but there is one older than I. Go to the Toad in Cardiganshire and ask him your question ; perhaps he will be able to help you.'

The Eagle thanked the Thrush and set off on his journey to Cardiganshire. He didn't get there until the afternoon, and he found the old Toad sitting on a lily leaf in the middle of a muddy pond, blinking his old eyes in the bright afternoon sunshine.

THE EAGLE AND THE OWL

'Good afternoon, Mr Toad,' said the Eagle; 'I have been advised to come to you by my good friend Mr Thrush.'

'Oh, yes,' grunted the Toad in his strange harsh voice; 'and how can I help you?'

The Eagle explained and then waited for the Toad to speak. It was nearly half an hour before the Toad uttered a word; he was very very old and was busy thinking about something else anyway. The Eagle didn't like to remind him of the question he had asked, so he just folded his great wings and sat there, waiting. At last the Toad remembered what he had been asked.

'I only eat dust,' he said, and then he was quiet again. It was another half an hour before he continued, but still the Eagle waited patiently. 'And I never eat half enough dust to satisfy me. Do you see those hills over there?'

The Eagle nodded; he was afraid to say anything in case this might encourage the Toad to wait another half an hour before speaking again.

'I remember,' said the Toad, 'when the earth there was flat, and I have eaten as much earth as is contained in all those hills during my lifetime, and yet I eat less than a grain of dust a day lest all the dust of the earth may be consumed before I die. I am so old I do not even remember ever being young, and yet I know that the Owl is yet older than I am. That's all I can tell you, young man.'

The old Eagle smiled to hear himself called a young man.

'Why did you say you wanted to know the age of the Owl?' asked the Toad. 'I forget, I forget.'

'I want to marry her,' said the Eagle, 'but I had first to be sure she is old and wise.'

'Marry her!' grunted the Toad. 'Marry that old grey hag who cries too-whit too-whoo in the night, frightening children and keeping everyone awake ! Ah well, rather you than I,' and he shut his eyes and went off to sleep.

The Eagle might have been annoyed at the Toad's description of his wife-to-be, but at last he had been convinced that the Owl was old enough to make him a suitable wife and he was too pleased about this to feel cross with the funny old Toad.

' Thank you, Mr Toad,' he said ; ' thank you very much, and I hope you'll come to the wedding.'

So the Eagle proposed to the Owl and was accepted. Most of the old folk of the country came to the ceremony including, of course, Mr Stag, Mr Salmon and Mr Thrush. Mr Toad did not come for, to tell the truth, he had lost his wedding invitation, and had forgotten all about the wedding anyway.

King of the Birds ❧

THERE was a time when the birds of Wales decided they ought to have a king, so they gathered together amid the hills in order to choose their monarch. Never was there such a gathering of feathered folk ! They came from as far as Flintshire and Denbighshire in the north and Glamorganshire and Pembrokeshire in the south. There were large birds and medium-sized birds and tiny birds ; and such a chattering and a whistling and a singing had never been heard in one place before.

' How are we going to choose our king ? ' asked a fat little Thrush of his neighbour.

' By vote, I suppose,' replied a gaily coloured Kingfisher, the blue and green of his wings glittering like turquoise and emerald jewels in the sunshine.

' That would be very difficult,' said a cheeky black and white Magpie, ' there are so many from which to choose. It would be better to make me king without voting and thus save a lot of fuss.'

' W-what a s-silly idea ! ' said a Reed-bunting, stuttering a little as all the buntings do.

' Our king must be the bird who can fly the highest, surely,' suggested the Chaffinch, a sensible bird who knew he was never likely to be crowned.

The Skylark, who naturally fancied his chance, seconded this idea, and there was a general chorus of twittering in agreement.

Some of the water birds like the ducks, swans and herons, however, voiced their disapproval because they were unable to fly to any very great height.

The Wren, tiniest bird of those present and speaking in a very loud voice for so small a body, was the noisiest in support of the Chaffinch's suggestion.

'I don't know why you are so pleased with the idea,' said the stately Eagle, ' for you can hardly expect to fly as high as many another bird.'

' You, for example ? ' asked the Wren.

' Well, yes,' said the Eagle, ' for I am strong and my wings are big, quite apart from the fact that I live in the mountains and have to fly to great heights every day.'

' We'll see, we'll see,' said the Wren.

The contest began almost immediately. Without being seen by anyone, the impudent Wren hopped on to the Eagle's back and, so light was he, the Eagle never even knew he was there.

Up into the clear blue sky flew the birds, and one by one they dropped out of the contest, tired and exhausted. Up still went the Hawk, the Skylark and the Eagle. Then the Hawk dropped back and flew down to earth to rest. Soon after, the Skylark tired and, with a disappointed flutter of his wings, followed the Hawk to the ground, leaving the Eagle still flying triumphantly up and up and up.

' The Eagle is king ! ' shouted the birds ; ' the Eagle is king ! '

They were pleased about this because the Eagle looked and behaved as a king should do, and they could be proud of him.

Exhausted by his tremendous effort, the Eagle stopped flying upwards and was about to turn on his downward flight when the Wren hopped off his back and, not having had to fly at all so far, he was full of energy and flew without effort a few yards higher

KING OF THE BIRDS

than the exhausted Eagle. Try as he could, the Eagle was too
tired to fly any higher, and both the birds began their return
journey to the ground. On the way down the Eagle, suddenly
overcome with anger at the trick the Wren had played on him,
waited until the Wren had caught him up, and then he threw
himself upon the little bird, hurling him to the grassy earth. The
Wren was not much hurt but he found he had lost half the
feathers of his tail, and that is why to this day he is called Y Dryw
Bach Cwta, the cut-tailed Wren.

'I flew the highest, I flew the highest,' chanted the Wren,
too pleased with himself to worry about the lost feathers of his
tail, ' and I am now your king.'

The other birds were dismayed. It was true the Wren had
flown higher than the Eagle, but how could they possibly submit
to being ruled over by the smallest and cheekiest of their number ?
They were so ashamed at the thought that some of them began
to weep.

' Our new king will have to die,' announced the pinkish-
brown Jay in his harsh voice.

' Yes, for his trickery, he must die,' echoed the birds.

' We can drown him in our tears,' said the bearded Tit,
nodding his blue-grey head and waggling his black moustache.

' Yes, drown him, drown him,' echoed the birds.

While the Wren shouted loudly that they couldn't do this to
their new king, some of the birds found a large pan in which to
drown the Wren, and as by now they were every one of them
in tears, it was arranged that one by one they should weep these
tears into it that they might all have a hand in the death of the
little king. Up they came to the rim of the pan, one by one,
and drip, drip, drip into the vessel fell their little bird tears. It
was nearly full when the Owl's turn came. The poor old Owl,

61

never a graceful bird, clumsily climbed on to the edge of the pan and, before he knew quite what had happened, he had knocked it over and the tears that had taken so long to collect were spilled upon the ground. Immediately the other birds set on him, pecking him fiercely for his carelessness. Even today the birds set on the Owl, and perhaps that is why he only dares to show himself at night when they are asleep. That, at any rate, is one legend about the Owl.

The Wren, who had been quite sure somehow that he would not be killed, was delighted with the Owl for his clumsiness. He had been badly frightened when he realised what his new subjects intended doing with him, and now he decided he had better make an effort to calm them down.

' Friends,' he called out, ' I am sorry I have made you angry and you must know I never really wanted to be your king. It was a joke on my part. The Eagle is obviously far better suited to be king than I am. He is bigger and more handsome and probably much cleverer. I therefore have much pleasure in resigning my position and giving up my throne to the brave Eagle.'

The birds clapped and whistled. The Eagle accepted the Wren's offer, although he did so in a sulky manner for he still felt cross. Everyone was pleased, not least among them the Wren, for even though the Eagle was always to be King of the Birds, the little Wren would always be able to tell his family how he had once been king even if it was only for a few hours.

Blodeuedd and the Slaying of Llew ✌❧

LLEW was a handsome youth and he had an uncle, called Gwydion, who loved him dearly. Because of a disagreement an evil old woman laid a curse on Llew, and this is what she told Gwydion :

'He, Llew Llaw Gyffes, your nephew, shall never have a wife of the race that is now on this earth.'

'You are a wicked woman,' shouted back Gwydion, 'but I shall see to it that he has a wife in spite of the curse you have laid upon him.'

Gwydion went to see his lord and friend whose name was Math and, with sorrow in his heart for Llew, explained what had happened.

'Cease your worrying,' said Math, 'for you and I between us, sharing our knowledge of magic and wisdom, can by enchantment make such a wife for Llew that he could not find throughout the land. We will make him a wife out of flowers.'

They went together into the country and there they gathered the flowers of the oak, the golden broom and the laced meadowsweet. Uttering magic spells over the massed blossoms, Gwydion and Math conjured forth a fair and lovely maiden whom they called Blodeuedd, meaning 'Flowers'.

When Llew saw her, he loved Blodeuedd instantly, and soon they were married.

For a time they lived together happily but, one day, Llew went to visit Math, leaving his lovely wife at home in their

63

castle. She was busy at her household tasks when she heard the blast of a horn and, going to the window, she saw a stag running by, followed by dogs and huntsmen.

'Go,' she said to her page, 'and ask whose men it is that are outside.'

'Madam,' said the lad on his return, 'it is Gronw, lord of Penllyn, and his huntsmen.'

All day Gronw hunted the stag and at night, on his way back, Blodeuedd, out of hospitality, invited him and his tired huntsmen into the castle for rest and food. Alas, it would have been better for Llew had they never met, for as soon as Blodeuedd and Gronw set eyes on each other they fell in love. It was not long before the wicked pair began to plot Llew's death that they might be free to marry each other.

'Llew is enchanted,' said Blodeuedd, 'and I know that his death can only come about in some special and secret way.'

'Find out exactly how,' counselled Gronw, 'and then we can make our plans.'

By the time Llew returned home, Gronw had gone. Glad to be back with his wife, Llew looked forward to a few hours' pleasant conversation but Blodeuedd scarcely seemed to listen to his words and remained quite silent, until at last Llew said to her :

'What is the matter ? You are so quiet and sad. Are you not well ? '

'I am thinking,' she answered, 'and I am worried. What if you should die before me ? How unhappy I should be ! '

'I thank you for your loving care of me,' said Llew to his false wife, 'but you have little need to worry. It is not easy for me to be killed.'

'To put my mind at rest then,' Blodeuedd said, 'tell me in what way you may be killed.'

BLODEUEDD AND THE SLAYING OF LLEW

' Certainly, my love,' he replied. ' I can only be slain by a spear that has taken a year to make, and work on that spear must only be done on Sundays while the people are in church. And that is not all. I cannot be slain in a house nor yet outside it. I cannot be slain on horseback nor yet on foot.'

' Why then, how can you be slain ? ' asked Blodeuedd.

' A bath would have to be made for me,' said Llew, ' on a river bank, and it would have to be covered with a thatched frame ; then a goat would have to be brought and put beside the tub. I should have to place one foot on the back of this goat and the other on the edge of the tub. In such a position and under such conditions only can I be slain. You see how little cause you have to worry.'

' Indeed,' said Blodeuedd, ' your death can most easily be avoided.'

She sent to Gronw the news she had learnt with directions how to make the spear. At the end of the year, having worked on it only on Sundays when the people were in church, Gronw had it ready.

' My lord,' then said Blodeuedd to Llew, ' you remember how you once told me of the position in which you can be slain. I am curious to know exactly how you would do this. If I prepare you a covered bath by the river, will you show me ? '

Llew agreed to do so, and Blodeuedd sent word to Gronw to be close at hand. She made the bath ready and invited Llew to enter it, which he did. She sent for a goat, and had it placed at the side of the bath.

' Now,' she said to her husband, ' show me just how you would balance on the goat and the tub.'

Llew arose out of the bath and balanced carefully on the edge of the tub then, raising his right foot, he placed it on the back of the goat. At that moment Gronw came out of his hiding-place near by and, lifting the spear, he aimed it straight at the poised body of Llew. It hit him in the side, the shaft broke off and the head of the spear stayed in the wound ; with a terrible scream, Llew turned into an eagle and flew away out of sight.

When the dreadful news reached Math and Gwydion, great was their grief.

' I shall not rest,' said Gywdion, ' until I have found my beloved nephew.'

' My blessing shall go with you,' said Math.

For days and weeks and months, Gwydion searched for Llew, until he came to a house where the swineherd told him of a certain sow in the herd who, as soon as the sty was opened, wandered off on her own, and no-one knew where she went.

' I am interested in this sow,' said Gwydion. ' May I be present at the sty tomorrow when you open it ? '

The swineherd readily agreed, although he thought it a strange request ; and early next morning Gwydion went with him. The swineherd opened the sty and out sprang the sow setting off at great speed. Gwydion followed her upstream, across fields, over hills, until they reached a quiet valley. There the sow stopped and began to feed under an oak tree. Gwydion moved nearer and saw that the sow was feeding on rotten flesh and maggots. He looked up at the tree and there, at the very top, sat an eagle who, when he shook himself, showered down the rotten flesh and worms that the sow was eating.

' That eagle must be Llew,' murmured Gwydion to himself. He began to sing, and this is what he sang :

' Between two lakes an oak there grows
Sheltered from the wind that blows,

BLODEUEDD AND THE SLAYING OF LLEW

I think I do not tell a lie—
My nephew Llew rests there on high.'

Hearing this, the eagle flew lower and sat on a branch in the middle of the tree.

Gwydion sang again.

' Grows an oak on upland plain
Not warmed by sun, nor wet by rain ;
May his hardships soon be o'er
And Llew restored to us once more.'

And the eagle flew down until he was on the lowest branch of the tree.   Then Gwydion sang :

' Grows an oak upon a steep
Where a lord his home doth keep,
If I do not speak falsely,
Llew will come on to my knee.'

This time the eagle flew right down and alighted on Gwydion's knee.   Gwydion took a magic wand from his pocket and lightly touched the bird, who immediately turned back into the proper likeness of Llew.   But, because of the wound he had received and the flesh he had lost while an eagle, Llew was now a pitiful sight, nothing but skin and bone.   Gwydion and his nephew embraced each other warmly and soon Llew was back in Math's castle where the best physicians attended him.   When he was quite recovered, Llew made plans with Math and Gwydion for revenge on Gronw and Blodeuedd.

' The sooner I can be revenged,' he said, ' the better pleased I shall be.'

Llew sought out Gronw, leaving Gwydion to find Blodeuedd. He had a message from Gronw asking him if he would accept gold or silver for the injury done to him, but this Llew refused.

'Let him go,' Llew told the messenger sent him by Gronw, 'to the spot by the river where I was when he aimed the spear at me, and there let me aim a spear at him, for surely this will be fair.'

Gronw agreed to these terms, but when the two of them met by the river bank Gronw begged a favour of Llew.

'What I did to you,' he said, 'was done because of a woman, so will it please you to let me place a stone between you and me before you strike a blow with your spear?'

'You may do that,' said Llew. Gronw took a large stone and set it between them. Llew took aim at him with the spear and it pierced through the stone and then through Gronw; and so Llew had his revenge and ruled again in his own land.

Meanwhile Blodeuedd, hearing that Gwydion was approaching her castle with his soldiers, gathered together her maidens and fled to the mountains. They were very frightened and, anxious to see how near was the oncoming enemy, they kept their heads constantly turned behind them; thus they fell backwards into a lake and, with the exception of Blodeuedd, were drowned. Gwydion soon captured her.

'I shall not slay you, Blodeuedd,' he said. 'Death is too good for such a one as you. I shall let you go in the form of a bird and, so great is the harm you did to Llew, I forbid you to show yourself in the daylight. Between you and other birds shall there always be enmity. You shall not lose your name but it shall be changed to Blodewedd.'

Touching the lovely but evil maiden with his magic wand, Gwydion turned her into an owl, the owl's name being 'Blodewedd' or flower-face which, as you will agree, is a good description of that round-faced bird. And that is another legend about the owl.

68

March's Ears 🌿

K ING MARCH, lord of Castell-march in Lleyn, had a secret ;
and it was a secret he shared only with his barber. Indeed
it would have been difficult to keep such a thing from his barber,
for the truth was, and the secret was, King March had the ears of
a horse ! He usually managed to keep these hidden but, of
course, he was unable to hide them from the man who cut
his hair and shaved his face. So ashamed was the King of his
deformity, he made the barber swear never to tell a living soul.

' If,' said King March, ' you breathe one word of this to
anyone, I shall immediately order your execution.'

The keeping of a secret can be a difficult matter, and the
knowledge he had, together with the threat of death should
that knowledge be revealed, began to weigh heavily upon the
barber. He worried about it, and the worry made him ill.
He had to call in the doctor. This doctor was a wise and clever
man ; having first examined him and then questioned him, he
said to his patient :

' My good man, if you go on like this you will not recover
from your sickness. It is my belief that you are slowly being killed
by a secret. Rest in bed will not cure you, nor any medicine
which I could give you. To tell your secret is the way to relief.'

' Alas,' replied the barber, ' it is true I have a secret, but it is
something I can tell to no-one.'

'Then tell it to the ground,' advised the doctor, 'but keep it to yourself no longer.'

The barber arose from his bed, and left the palace. When he came to some marshy ground in a lonely spot a few miles away, he went down on his knees and, putting his mouth close to the ground, he whispered :

'King March has horse's ears.'

As soon as he had shared his secret, even though it was only with the ground, the barber felt better ; and where he had whispered the secret words, there grew up some particularly fine reeds.

One day, a little later, certain pipers from a place called Maelgwn Gwyned were on the way to a feast that was to be held at King March's palace, when they passed the spot where the barber had confided his secret to the ground. There they saw the fine reeds growing tall and straight.

'These reeds would make good pipes,' said one of the pipers. So the pipers cut the reeds and used them for their pipes.

'We'll make sweet music with these for the King at the feast,' said another of the pipers. And they went on their way.

That night when the feasting was at its height, King March called for music.

'Let the pipers play,' he ordered; 'I am in the mood for music.'

The pipers came forward and proudly lifted their fine new pipes to their lips. But when they blew the first few notes of what was meant to be the King's favourite tune, a terrible thing happened. The pipes all sang out together :

'Horse's ears for King March ! Horse's ears for King March ! '

The pipers lowered their pipes with horror and gazed in terror at the King whose face was terrible to see. The secret

70

The eagle flew down until he was on the lowest branch of the tree

he had tried so hard to keep was now out, proclaimed thus for everyone to hear. In a voice of thunder, he bellowed :

'Let every piper go instantly to his death,' and he gestured to his soldiers who stood on guard at his side.

One of the pipers, however, a man of courage, stepped forward before the soldiers could grab him.

'If it please you, sir,' he spoke out, 'it is not our fault. The pipes are bewitched. Here, try for yourself. See, they refuse to play any tune,' and he held out his pipe towards the King.

King March was a just man but hasty in temper, and perhaps unnecessarily sensitive about his ears. He took the offered pipe and lifted it to his lips. With careful fingering he tried to play a little jig of which he was fond.

'Horse's ears for King March,' sang the pipe. 'Horse's ears for King March !'

Quietly the King laid down the pipe and ordered the soldiers to release the pipers. The heavy burden of the secret was his no more ; he even began to feel light-hearted about it. No-one had laughed at him. Most of those present looked quite sympathetic. Later, when the barber confessed that he had told the secret to the ground where the reeds grew from which the pipes had been made, the King was almost able to laugh a little himself.

And that was the origin of a Welsh saying : 'That is gone on horns or pipes,' meaning that a supposed secret is most certainly a secret no more.

The Young Man who Married a Fairy ✌➠

THERE was a young man, Evan, of Caernarvonshire who, on long, still summer evenings when the moon shone white and cold in a starlit sky, had an unusual hobby. Better than reading a book in the house, or talking with his friends or walking in the country, he liked to go into the fields to watch the fairies dance, and to hear them sing.

Such gay dances they danced and such sweet songs they sang, this young man often thought he would like to watch and listen to them for ever and ever. Of course, they always danced in fairy rings and they did not always choose the same field, but usually it was some distance away from the house where Evan lived. You can imagine his pleasure, therefore, when one evening he found them dancing in a small green field very near his house, and on this particular evening not only were the dances gayer and the music sweeter than ever, but the fairies who were dancing and singing were the most beautiful Evan had ever seen.

Very quietly, so that he should not be seen or heard, Evan crept close to the fairy ring. The fairies danced hand in hand, round and round in the ring, and some of them had hair as gold as buttercups, some of them hair as black as the raven's wing, some of them hair as brown as the hazel nut and some of them hair as red as the fire flame.

It was then that Evan fell in love ; one of the fairies was so

72

One of the fairies was so beautiful he could not take his eyes off her

beautiful he could not take his eyes off her. Her skin was like cream, her cheeks were flushed like the petal of the wild rose, her hair, paler gold than the buttercup and nearer to the primrose, turned to silver when the moon shone on it. Her voice, which Evan heard when she swung past him, was clear and sweet, the notes reaching high up to the sky like a nightingale's, while her small feet skimmed the green grass as gently as the breeze rustles the tall tree tops. Evan knew he would never love anyone else, and he determined to have her for his wife.

Suddenly, when the gaiety of the fairies was at its height, he rushed into the ring, seized the primrose-haired fairy in his strong arms, dragged her out of the magic circle and began to run as fast as his legs would carry him. Faintly, and very far away, he could hear the dismayed cries of the fairies who were left behind. He did not stop to look round, but ran on until he reached his house. Then he carefully placed the fairy in a softly cushioned chair where she sat, curled up, looking at him out of frightened eyes that were as blue as a summer sky.

'Do not be frightened,' said Evan. 'I love you, and want you for my wife. Won't you speak to me?'

The fairy shook her head.

'Do you not think you could grow to love me?' went on Evan.

Still the fairy gazed at him without speaking.

'I would do anything to win your love,' said Evan. 'Won't you please stay here with me?'

Then the fairy spoke, and her voice filled the room with such sweetness that Evan felt quite dizzy.

'No,' she said, 'I cannot love you for you are a human, and I do not want to stay. I want to return to my own people. Please let me go.'

But Evan refused to listen to her pleading; he had never wanted anything as much in his life as he wanted to marry this fairy.

After much argument, she at last agreed to stay as she could see Evan would never allow her to return to her own people.

'If I stay,' she said, 'I will not stay as your wife but only as your serving-maid.'

Evan was disappointed to hear this, but to have her near him would be better than not having her at all; and perhaps later on he could persuade her to become his wife. He was further disappointed when he heard what the fairy said next.

'And I shall only stay as your serving-maid if you can find out my name,' she added.

'Do fairies have special names?' asked Evan, 'or names like Welsh girls?'

'Find out,' said the fairy.

'Dilys, Morfydd, Sian, Blodwen?' guessed Evan.

The fairy chuckled, and shook her head.

'Gwyneth, Olwen, Mari, Eluned, Mai?' he guessed, but still the fairy shook her head.

74

THE YOUNG MAN WHO MARRIED A FAIRY

Evan spent the whole evening trying to guess her name, and started again next morning.

' Ceridwen, Rhiannon, Myfanwy, Ceinwen, Branwen . . . ? '

At every name he suggested the fairy shook her head so that he began to think he was never going to find out what it was. He had to go to market that day so, after a few more tries, he gave up and told the fairy he would guess again when he returned that night.

On his way back from market he happened to see, huddled together on a mossy bank, a group of fairies deep in conversation. He thought he recognised among them one or two of the dancers of the night before.

' Now I wonder,' said Evan to himself, ' if they are discussing some way of rescuing their sister. Perhaps they will mention her name and then my worries will be over.'

There was a ditch running alongside the bank, and into this Evan dropped, creeping along in it until he was under the group of fairies. Without being seen, he managed to overhear their conversation.

' It is a terrible thing that has happened,' moaned one of the fairies.

' Terrible, indeed ! ' said another, whose long black hair streamed down her back almost to her feet.

' Oh, Penelope, Penelope ! ' sighed a third, ' why did you run away with a mortal man ? '

' Penelope,' murmured Evan to himself; ' so that's her name.

He couldn't get back to his house quickly enough, and when he reached it he flung open the door and saw his fairy still sitting in the chair where he had left her. She smiled at him as he came in.

' Hello, Evan,' she said, ' and do you know my name yet ? '

' Yes, Penelope, indeed I do,' said Evan triumphantly.

The fairy began to cry, rocking herself to and fro in her unhappiness. When she had finished weeping she dried her eyes and, clasping her hands together, she said :

' Oh, Evan, who revealed my name to you, who revealed my name ? '

Evan told her how he had overheard her sisters talking, and when Penelope heard this she knew she must keep her bargain. In spite of Evan's persuasions, she still refused to marry him. However, there was no woman for miles around who kept a house so clean, bought food so economically and cared for a small farm so well. Everything she did, she did well, and Evan never knew whether or not she wove a fairy spell over the animals, but the cows gave more milk, the hens laid more eggs and the pigs provided better bacon than ever before.

The young man ought to have been the happiest—for he was fast becoming the wealthiest—man in the neighbourhood. But he knew he would not be really happy until Penelope consented to be his wife.

The months went by until one day, perhaps because she was weary of Evan's pleas or perhaps because she had by now grown truly fond of him, Penelope agreed to marry him.

' I shall marry you on one condition,' she said, ' and that is, should you ever strike me with iron, I shall be allowed to go free and return to the fairy folk.'

Evan thought this a strange request, but he agreed readily ; he was delighted that Penelope was at last going to marry him.

They were married, and they lived happily together for many years. One summer's day Evan decided to go to Caernarvon Fair. He went into one of his fields to catch a young filly he wanted to sell at the Fair, but this filly was high-spirited and, in spite of his efforts, Evan could not manage to get near enough to her to put on the bridle.

'Penelope, my dear,' he called out, 'will you please come and help me with this bad filly. I cannot put the bridle on her.'

'Coming, Evan,' replied Penelope, and she left her children (she and Evan now had a large family) playing in the kitchen. She ran across to the field where the filly was causing Evan so much trouble. With her help, Evan managed to get the horse into a corner and, making carefully towards her, he was about to bridle her when she turned and broke loose again.

Evan, tired now and thoroughly bad-tempered, lifted the bridle high in the air and threw it with all his might at the naughty filly. Alas and alack, his aim was bad and, instead of hitting the filly, the bridle hit his wife, the iron part of it striking her on the face. Immediately Penelope vanished. One moment she was there, standing in the field and laughing to see her husband so cross, and the next moment she had gone completely. Poor Evan looked everywhere for her but could find no trace. He had struck Penelope with iron quite accidentally, and she had returned to her own people as she had said she would do.

Evan never saw her again, but sometimes he would hear her sweet voice outside his window at night, asking him if the children were well, warm and cared for. They always were; Evan loved them dearly as each one of them looked like the lovely fairy wife he had adored. And these children's children and their children's children were ever afterwards called *Pellings* after their fairy ancestress Penelope.

The Legend of Bala Lake ✍➍

IT is said that sometimes, during harvest time on quiet moon-light nights, a boatman rowing on the still waters of Bala Lake may see through the water the ruined towers of a palace. And if such a boatman were to stop his rowing and, resting his oars, listen carefully, it is even possible he would hear a feeble voice saying, 'Vengeance will come!'

Vengeance indeed did come to the prince who once lived in the palace that now lies under the waters of Bala. This prince was a cruel and vain man who treated the workers and farmers who lived on his land very badly, neither caring if they went hungry nor if they had clothes enough to wear. He only lived to enjoy himself, and no money was spared to this end.

Often when he was merry-making in his luxurious gardens, where there grew every sort of rare and lovely flower and tree, the prince would hear a voice that floated towards him from the air, and which only he seemed able to hear.

'Vengeance will come,' whispered the voice in his ear, 'vengeance will come!'

But the prince always laughed when he heard these ominous words, and told himself that someone was playing a trick on him, and that it was all nonsense anyway. Indeed he was so contemptuous of the threat that one day, when the voice had uttered 'Vengeance will come!' in louder tones than usual, the prince decided there and then to have the most extravagant

78

party at his palace that he had ever had. His first grandson had just been born and that was to be the excuse, if excuse be needed, for such rejoicing, drinking, dancing and merriment as had never before been seen in the land. He began to make plans for this. As he ordered the great barrels of wine and the oxen that were to be roasted whole for the feast, the prince had no thought for the men outside the palace gates who were starving or for their children who were dying for want of milk. There would be no dancing or singing in these homes. But neither did he think of that when he ordered the presence of a poor harper from over the hills to play for his guests.

This harper was, of course, delighted to be asked ; although he played his harp with great skill, he did not make much money and he hoped the wealthy prince would pay him well for the evening's entertainment. He had heard of the magnificence and luxury of the prince's palace, but never had he imagined such splendour as met his eyes in the huge hall where he played for the ladies and gentlemen who were the prince's friends. The silks and satins of their clothes glittered in the light of the flaming torches that blazed from the walls, the long wooden tables were heavy with foods of every description, and hundreds of the prince's servants poured the ruby wine endlessly from big silver jugs into tall silver goblets.

As the harper lovingly played his harp, the guests danced to his music hour after hour. At about midnight, however, there was a lull in the dancing while the dancers refreshed themselves, and the old harper sat quietly in a corner of the hall. Suddenly he heard a voice whispering to him ; he turned to see who was speaking but there was no-one there. Again the voice spoke. indeed it almost seemed to sing. ' Vengeance,' it said, ' vengeance ! ' Again the harper turned, and this time he saw a little

79

bird hovering above him who seemed to beckon him with its wings. Without thinking, he arose and, pushing his way through the noisy crowd, he followed the bird.

It was only when he reached the palace gates that the old harper hesitated. ' How foolish,' he told himself, ' to leave a good job for which I have not yet been paid, just to follow a little bird.'

The bird continued to flap its wings and urge him on, and continued to sing sadly, ' Vengeance, vengeance ! '

The harper felt impelled to follow it. On they went, over bogs, across streams, through thickets, the bird always hovering just in front and leading the harper along the easiest and safest paths. If, for one moment, the harper hesitated, the bird began to sing again the same mournful, ' Vengeance, vengeance ! '

At last they reached the top of a high hill, a long distance from the palace, and here the harper sank to the ground, tired out. This time, when he listened for the bird's warning voice, he could hear it no more. He heard nothing save the rippling murmur of a nearby brook. Again he told himself how foolish he had been to let himself be led away from the palace feast. It was perhaps an hour since he had first heard the cry of the bird. If he hurried back perhaps his absence would not have been noticed, and he could start to play again for the next dance.

Tired though he was, the old harper got to his feet and tried to find his way back to the palace but, without the bird to guide him, he soon lost his way. He wandered about the hillside, until it became obvious that he would have to wait until daybreak before continuing his journey. As he curled up in the bracken to try and get some sleep, he murmured to himself :

' Had it not been for that wretched bird, I should not now be in this sorry state. I've missed the end of the feast, I've not been paid for my work and, even worse, I have left my harp behind in the palace.'

But, in the morning, when the harper awoke and turned his eyes towards the palace in the valley below, his gratitude to the little bird knew no bounds. Vengeance had come indeed! There, where once stood a magnificent palace, and where only the night before a cruel and oppressive prince had danced and laughed with his friends, was now a large expanse of calm water shining in the morning sun. And, floating on the face of those waters which today are known as Bala Lake, was the old man's beloved harp.

The Legend of Llangorse Lake ❧

IN the county of Breconshire, not far from the present county town of Brecon, was once a large and flourishing city, and the king of the district was worried about this town. He sent for one of his most loyal and trusted servants, and said to him :

' Mervyn, it has come to my ears that this city, in which dwell many of my subjects, is a wicked place where the citizens spend their time in riotous living. This may only be a rumour, but I wish you to go there and report to me the truth of the matter. If it is indeed such a place as I have heard, it shall be destroyed ; I refuse to have the good name of my kingdom ruined.'

Mervyn left the palace, and journeyed to the city on his master's errand. He arrived at the city gates in the evening. There were no guards on duty and he walked through without a challenge, although he could hear sounds of drinking and laughter in the guard-room. The city streets were full of dancing, rioting people who jostled Mervyn as he slowly passed among them. No-one greeted him or took much notice of him except to jeer at his solemn looks, and no-one offered him food to eat or lodging for the night.

The farther into the town Mervyn went, the worse became the wild scenes. Wearied by the noise and deeply shocked by what he had seen, he at last sought rest in a poor part of the town. The door of one of the little houses was open so he entered, only to find that the family had all apparently gone off to enjoy themselves. The house seemed empty but, as the king's servant stood there undecided what he should do next, he heard crying, and in the far corner of the room he saw a cradle in which lay a small baby.

Mervyn sat down by the cradle, and began to rock it.

' There, there, little one,' he soothed, ' go to sleep,' and as the baby happily closed its eyes and slept, Mervyn found the tears running down his own cheeks at the thought that this innocent and neglected babe must perish with the guilty ones of this wicked city. He stayed the night with the child, amusing him in his waking moments with his jewelled gloves whose bright colours attracted the baby's eye.

At daybreak Mervyn left that he might reach the palace early and make his report to the king. He was outside the town when he was startled to hear a rumble like thunder, followed by wild cries and shrieks. These at last died down until he could hear now only what sounded like the lapping of waves. Then there was silence. It was still dark and Mervyn, not able to see what had happened, decided to continue on his way. However, it was cold and, looking for his gloves which he usually kept tucked in his belt when he wasn't wearing them, he found one was missing. Then he remembered that he must have left this in the baby's cradle. It was a nuisance but he'd have to go back for it ; the gloves had been a present from the king and Mervyn prized them highly.

It was not long before he reached the place where the city should have been but there, instead of the streets, houses and gardens, lay a vast sheet of water on which one tiny object was sailing. The wind gradually wafted this towards Mervyn until he was able to recognise it as the cradle in which lay, not only his jewelled glove, but the baby himself, alive and well and crowing with delight to see his friend of the night before.

Mervyn carried the child to the king, and showed him as the one innocent soul who had been saved from the wretched and evil city that now lay under the waters of the Lake called Llangorse.

The Cruel Giant ✎

THERE was once a giant who lived in a castle in an isolated spot amid the mountains of Wales. This giant was a cruel, ugly man with wild red hair and a temper to match it; and he had a daughter. But this daughter, whose name was Mair, was small and lovely and gentle; and she hated the father who treated her without love or kindness. Her mother had died when she was a baby, and Mair led a lonely life in the cold, damp castle. As she cooked, washed and cleaned for her father, she was kept very busy and she had little or no time for the usual pleasures and hobbies of young people—and anyway she knew no young people with whom to share such joys.

You can imagine her delight, therefore, when one day, as she was picking mushrooms in a nearby field, she saw a young man on a horse approach her. Any young man would have been a welcome sight for a girl as lonely as Mair, but this young man was handsome and sweetly spoken. He had lost his way and, after Mair had given him directions to the nearest village, he stayed a while and talked to her. Before he left, he told her he would like to see her again.

'Do not come to the castle, young man,' warned Mair. 'My father is a fierce giant and there would be no welcome for you there.'

'Then I will meet you in the fields tomorrow at the same time,' promised the young man. 'My name is Idwal.'

'And mine is Mair,' replied the girl shyly.

It was the beginning of many such meetings, and fortunately for them the giant never saw his daughter and Idwal together. After some weeks Idwal told Mair that he loved her and wished to marry her. Mair said she returned his love, and that she would dearly like to be his wife.

'I shall go now and find your father to ask his permission to marry you,' said Idwal, kissing her on her soft pink cheek.

'No, no,' cried out Mair, 'that will never do. He would never consent; he would probably kill you for asking. He is a terrible man. You cannot know how terrible a man he is,' and she began to weep.

'Dry your tears,' comforted Idwal. 'If he is so terrible, I shall not ask his permission. We will run away together now. Go to the castle and quickly pack your clothes My horse will willingly carry us both, and we shall be far away from this dreadful place before your father discovers you are missing.'

Mair agreed but, as she walked back to the castle, she wondered if escape would be as easy as Idwal had suggested. As she packed her clothes, her hands shaking with fear and excitement, she remembered something she had heard of the magical properties of certain of her father's possessions. She was sure he would come after her once he had discovered her absence and perhaps, who knew, these magic things would help to protect her from him. She tiptoed to the giant's bedroom and, from a chair by his bed, she took a comb, a razor and a small mirror. These she put into the pocket of her gown.

She joined Idwal in the field, and soon she was seated behind him on his horse, and they were away over the fields and beyond the hills.

The harper felt impelled to follow the little bird

THE CRUEL GIANT

Not long after they had gone, the giant called for his dinner. His deep voice boomed through the echoing castle.

' Mair, bring me my dinner ! Mair, bring me my dinner ! '

There was no reply, no clattering of dishes, no movement in the kitchen. Again the giant called, and still there was no answer. He arose and went to look for his daughter, his ugly face screwed up with anger. When he did not find her, he bellowed aloud with fury and struck his great fist so hard on the dining-room table that the table broke into two pieces.

Then he raced to the stables and saddled his huge black charger that was faster than any other horse in Wales. Already he had guessed that Mair had run away and, when he found the track of Idwal's horse, he realised that she probably had not gone alone. Now his fury knew no bounds. Any young man who had dared to steal his daughter should not be allowed to live, and when he brought the girl back to her home she should be made to suffer for such disgraceful behaviour. He dug his heels into the horse's flanks and faster, faster, faster, he rode after the runaway couple.

A few minutes later, Mair, clinging on tightly behind Idwal on his horse, happened to turn her head and saw her father only half a mile behind.

' It's my father, Idwal,' she moaned, ' close on our heels. I shall see if the magic comb will help us.'

She put her hand into her pocket and, withdrawing the comb, she threw it behind her with all the force she could muster. Immediately the comb turned into a rough tangled forest through which the giant was forced to cut and hack his way. This delayed him for several hours but, once he was through it and on his horse again, it was not long before Mair once more saw him riding furiously a little way behind them.

' It's my father, Idwal,' she moaned, ' close on our heels. I shall see if the magic razor will help us,' and, putting her hand in her pocket, she withdrew the razor and threw it behind her with all the force she could muster.

The razor became a steep mountain ridge through which the infuriated giant had to tunnel his way. With his huge hands he worked fast, shovelling out the earth like a burrowing mole. This time the delay was longer, but at last the giant worked his way through to the other side. On fled the lovers, always hoping the giant would fail to catch them up. But again, Mair, turning her head, saw her father plunging towards them on his foam-flecked horse.

'It's my father, Idwal,' she moaned, 'close on our heels. I shall see if the magic mirror will help us, for if it does not, alas, we are doomed,' and, taking the last magic object from her pocket, she threw it behind her with all the force she could muster.

The mirror instantly turned into a lake which, when the giant saw it, made him stamp and scream with fury. For the giant could not swim ! Nevertheless, so eager was he to catch his daughter, he plunged into the chilly waters and was drowned, and only his great black charger was there to mourn his death.

Thus did Mair and Idwal escape from the wicked giant, and they lived to enjoy many long and happy years together.

Elidorus in Fairyland ✤

ELIDORUS was studying in the monastery to be a priest but, like many another young boy, he did not like his books nor the hard work which learning them entailed. At first the monks of St David's were patient with him in the hope that he would soon improve but, as time went on and there were no signs of improvement, Elidorus received harsher treatment, and scarcely a day went by when he was not beaten for neglected or careless work.

At last, angry at what he considered was unfair treatment, Elidorus, only twelve years old, ran away. He daren't go home as he was sure his parents would send him back to the monks, so he went off into the countryside to hide. He found a perfect hiding-place under the hollow bank of a river, and there he curled himself up.

Every now and again he would peep out but, on seeing obvious signs of an organised search for him, he stayed where he was. Two whole days he was there, with nothing to drink or eat and no-one with whom to talk. He was quite pleased, therefore, when two tiny men appeared in front of him. He rubbed his eyes to see if he was dreaming but, no, there stood the two little men peering at him with beady black eyes. When one of them spoke he had a high-pitched, silvery-toned voice.

'If you will come with us,' he told Elidorus, ' we will lead you to a country full of delights and sports.'

Elidorus readily accepted this offer ; it was just the sort of
adventure he was looking for, and he couldn't have stayed where
he was for much longer.

The little men led the way down a path that ran underground
and was mossy with darkness, into a lovely country of rivers,
meadows, plains and hills whose full beauty it was difficult to
see as the sun never shone in this fairy place. Every day was
cloudy and every night was black as pitch ; there were no stars
or moon.

On the little men went, followed by Elidorus, until they
brought him to a palace and presented him to their King. The
King was tiny too, but like all the fairies Elidorus was to meet
he was perfectly proportioned, very fair-skinned and had hair
that fell, thick and curly, like a woman's to his shoulders. He
questioned Elidorus for many hours, and must have been satisfied with his answers for he passed him on to his son as a companion of his own age.

Elidorus soon settled down and became accustomed to the
tiny horses the little people rode and the tiny greyhounds they
kept for pets. It took him longer to get used to the food :
they never ate meat or fish but lived on milky dishes mixed
with saffron. And he soon learned that, above all else, the
fairy people loathed lies, and that it was unnecessary in their
land for anyone to take an oath. When any of them returned
from their journeyings to the human land above, they were
always full of scorn for human ambition and infidelity.

Elidorus frequently returned to his own land, sometimes by
the way he had first come and sometimes by another, but his
visits were short and secret. Only his mother saw him, and to
her he described the wonders of the lovely land where he now
passed most of his time. He also told her about the fairy people,

of their looks, ways and manners. On one of these visits he mentioned the abundance of gold to be found in fairyland.

' Even the balls with which the King's son plays are made of pure gold, Mother,' he said.

' Pure gold ! ' exclaimed his mother. ' How rich I should be if I possessed such a ball ! Elidorus, my son, could you not bring me a golden ball when next you come, for one, out of them all, could never be missed.'

At first Elidorus was shocked by this suggestion.

' Oh, no ! ' he replied, ' that would not be right. The little folk have been kind to me ; I could not repay their kindness by stealing one of their golden balls.'

Eventually Elidorus reluctantly agreed.

When he returned to the fairy land he stole a golden ball while playing with the King's son. The Prince's attention was on something else and Elidorus picked up the ball, put it under his jacket, and slipped out of the palace. He made for the path that led to the upper region, but he had not gone far when he heard the patter of little feet behind him and, turning his head, he saw he was being pursued by two of the fairy men. He started to run, hoping that his longer legs would take him out of reach but, when at last he arrived at his mother's house, weary and out of breath, the little men were still not very far behind him.

Elidorus flung open the door of the cottage and, as he did so, he tripped over the step and fell down. The golden ball rolled across the floor where it lay at his mother's feet. Like lightning the two little men raced into the room and pounced on the ball. As they turned to leave, they gave Elidorus such scornful glances that he was unable to look them in the face, and he hid his head in his arms.

' Oh, wretched traitor ! ' shouted one of the little men.

' Oh, false human ! ' shouted the other. And the two of them left the house.

Elidorus was filled with shame at his bad behaviour and regretful that he had listened to his mother's evil counsel, and he immediately went to find the underground passage to fairy-land that he might make his humble apologies to the King. But the river bank revealed no passage to him that day nor any other day. After a long time Elidorus realised that he would never be able to return to the land where he had been so happy, and he went back to the monks and continued his studies.

When he was older he became a learned monk himself, but he never forgot the joy he had experienced as a young boy in fairyland and, whenever he thought or spoke of it, he could not restrain his tears.

Years and years later, when he was a very old man, Elidorus was visited by David the Second, Bishop of St David's, who questioned him about his early fairy experiences, and Elidorus revealed that the fairy language was very like that of the Ancient Greeks.

This, the tale of Elidorus, is the very oldest written fairy tale we have in Wales, and it was recorded by Gerald of Wales in 1188.

Fairy Tricks 🌿

MOST fairies like to play tricks on unsuspecting mortals but certain fairies in Wales were especially fond of this form of amusement. These were known as the 'mischievous and wanton kind of fairies', and they lived in marshy places where the reeds grew or among the fern and heather of the moors. And here are three of the many tricks they were known to have played.

A man of Nevin was returning one night from the fair at the nearby town of Pwllheli. As he was jogging on his horse along the familiar road, he saw ahead of him a magnificent inn.

'That's funny,' he said to himself; 'many a time have I ridden along this road, and never before have I noticed this inn. There's something strange here.'

In spite of his doubts, and because he was tired and thirsty, he went towards the inn.

As he dismounted from his horse a servant came into the inn yard.

'May I stable my horse?' asked the man.

'Yes, certainly, sir,' replied the servant, 'I'll take him to the stables myself.'

There was something a little odd about the servant: he didn't look quite human and his voice sounded strange, but the man from Nevin handed over his horse and went into the inn where he asked for a pint of beer.

Never in his life had he tasted better beer. It was so delicious and so nicely served and the inn itself was so comfortable, he decided to go no farther that night.

' May I have a bed for the night ? ' he asked the innkeeper. There was something odd about the innkeeper too, although he answered civilly enough.

' Certainly, sir. I'll take you to your room now if you wish.'

And he led the man to a room fit for a king and left him there to sleep on a bed of swansdown, hung with the most rich and splendid tapestries.

But when he awoke next morning it only took him a second to discover he was a victim of a fairy trick. He found himself sleeping on a heap of ashes, and his horse tied to a post in the hedge !

Another trick the fairies were fond of playing was to tie down a sleeping mortal with ropes of finest gossamer.

Once a farmer's son, returning from a fair at Beddgelert, caught sight of some fairies dancing in a field, so he climbed over a stile and sat down quietly on a bank under the hedge. There he watched the little folk at play, and they were so pretty to see and so sweet to hear that the lad stayed there hour after hour until at last he fell asleep.

The fairies finished their dancing, and one of them drew the attention of the others to the mortal man lying fast asleep under the hedge. They crept up to him, bent on mischief. Then, giggling softly, they began to tie him down with gossamer ropes so that, had he awoken, he could not have moved. When that was done, they covered him with a gossamer sheet that made him invisible to the human eye. Then they left him.

The lad's family were frantic when the boy did not return

that night, and on the following day, with the help of their neighbours, they formed a search party. They looked everywhere for the missing boy, and many times they actually passed the spot where he lay but, of course, they were unable to see him

A day and a night passed before the fairies returned to release their victim. When he was free the boy was bewildered and he wandered about for hours not knowing where he was. Then his full senses returned to him and he found he was only a short distance from his home. There he was welcomed with open arms, even if his parents found his strange story a bit difficult to believe.

The fairies' cruellest trick was one they played on an old woman who lived in a wild spot among the mountains. There were more fairies than humans in this isolated spot, and they were on quite friendly terms with the old woman. From her point of view they were too friendly, because they were always borrowing things from her—a saucer of cream, a small jug of milk, a pat of butter and so on, and they always forgot to return them.

One day the old woman was out cutting turf for her fire when she met a few fairies who asked her if they might beg a piece of fresh bread off her.

'Oh, you fairies!' grumbled the old woman, 'I'm always lending you things, and what do I get out of it, I'd like to know. I tell you what, grant me two wishes—I know it's in your power —and you shall have a whole loaf of freshly baked bread in return.'

The fairies huddled together and whispered ; one of them laughed, and then another addressed himself to the old woman.

In a flash, the old woman's nose became half a yard longer!

'We have agreed to your request. You may have two wishes. What are they to be?'

Now the old woman had a stone on the wall near the door of her cottage that jutted out and got in her way.

'My first wish,' she said, 'is that the first thing I touch at the door shall break.'

She also had in the house a piece of flannel out of which she wanted to make herself a jacket, but unfortunately it was half a yard too short.

'My second wish,' she said, 'is that the first thing I put my hand on in the house shall be lengthened by half a yard.'

The fairies nodded their agreement but, as the old woman went off towards her cottage with the sack of turf on her back, she heard the echo of mocking fairy laughter.

As she neared her cottage door the poor old woman had the

misfortune to slip and, in trying to save herself, she put her hand, not on the stone she wanted broken, but on her knee which immediately snapped. Thus was her first wish wasted.

She limped into the house and, so great was the pain in her knee, she forgot her second wish and, feeling a tickle on her nose, she put her hand to it and in a flash it became half a yard longer ! Thus was her second wish wasted.

It is certain that she regretted having made her request to the fairies, and very unlikely that she ever lent them anything again.

The Girl and the Golden Chair 〜➤

M ARI lived in Caernarvonshire where her father was a farmer. Her parents were both hard-working ; indeed, they had to be in order to make a living out of their farm which was on a hillside where the soil was thin and poor.

Mari was a good and beautiful girl who did all she could to help her mother and father, the care of the sheep being her particular task.

At certain times of the year, such as at lambing when the sheep needed special attention, Mari visited them daily on the mountainside. She was a great knitter—she had been taught by her mother—and, as so many clever knitters today can knit and read or watch television at the same time, so Mari could knit as she walked, and this she did on her way to look after the sheep and on her way back home.

The fairies noticed that Mari, as well as being good and beautiful, was very industrious. They watched her from behind the hedges, they peeped at her from the flowery banks, and they studied her from the tops of little rocky crags on the mountainside, and always they saw her busy at her knitting. One day they decided to reward her.

Mari had reached the mountainside and was walking up a steep sheep track of a path when, looking up for a moment from the stocking she was just completing, she saw in front of her a glorious golden chair, beautifully wrought and glittering so that Mari had to shade her eyes for a moment as she gazed at it. She went up to it and gently touched it with her finger, wondering if she were imagining it, or if it would crumble away as she put her hand to it. But no, the golden chair was real enough and Mari, familiar with fairy ways, knew that it was intended as a gift for her. She also knew that fairy gifts had to be taken possession of at once. She put down her knitting on the short thick grass, and grasped the chair with both hands. But, pull as she might, the chair was too heavy for her to move.

She must get the chair home, but how was it to be done ? Mari sat down on the grass, gazed at the wonderful chair and thought. She was a long way from home, there was no–one who could help her and, if she left the chair and went for help, how was she to find her way back to it ? Her eyes rested on the discarded knitting that lay at her side, and she had an idea. If she tied the end of the ball of yarn to the chair and then un-rolled the ball as she made her way home, she could easily find her way back to the fairy gift. She got to her feet and knotted the end of the white yarn to the arm of the chair. With the ball in one hand and the stocking she had finished knitting in the other, Mari started to walk home, unravelling the ball as she went.

It was a big ball of yarn but it was surprising how soon it came to an end, long before Mari had the farm even in sight. But she was not outdone ; she tied the end of it to the yarn of the stocking and walked on again. Soon, however, the stocking, too, was completely unravelled. She was now only a short way from home and could see where her mother and father were working in the farmyard.

' Mother ! Father ! ' she called, but they did not hear her, and went on stolidly with their work.

Putting a stone on the end of her last bit of yarn, Mari raced home as if wings were attached to her feet. Breathless and excited, she told her story to her parents.

'Come quickly,' she urged, 'for you know what the fairies are like. If we do not claim the golden chair at once, it will have disappeared.'

Quickly the three of them made their way to the spot where Mari had placed the stone. But no stone could they find, and the only wool they could see was a bit of the raw material caught on a hedge where a sheep had pushed its way through.

For hours Mari and her parents searched for some sign of the yarn, but they could find none, and when darkness fell they had to give up and go home.

The next day they searched again, and this time Mari led them to the part of the mountainside where she thought she had first found the golden chair. They covered every inch of the ground, they climbed up every sheep track, they pushed their way through bracken and heather and brambles, but still they met with no success.

If only the yarn had been long enough the golden chair would have been Mari's. As it is, somewhere in those mountains of Caernarvonshire, the chair is still hidden. The fairies want someone to have it, but it is no use anyone going to search for it as Mari and her parents did, for whoever the fairies wish to possess it will come upon it one day, by accident, and let us hope when that happens the lucky person will either have enough yarn to guide the way back to it, or be strong enough to carry the golden chair home alone.

The Miller and the Fairies ≥►

IN North Wales there once lived a miller, and this miller was a very hard-working man but, in spite of the work he did, he was not a rich man and he and his good wife had a hard struggle to find enough money with which to buy their food and clothes.

They lived in a neat little house with a thatched roof, and the neat little house had a neat little garden in which the miller's wife grew roses, pansies and lilies-of-the-valley, and this little house was only a few steps away from the great mill whose huge wheel was turned by the water of the river that ran at its feet. In the mill, the miller stored the corn and the bags of flour.

Now at a certain time of the year the miller needed to dry his corn before he could grind it and, in order to dry it, he kept an enormous fire burning in the mill. Every night at this time of the year the miller stayed up late to tend to the fire, heaping shiny black pieces of coal upon it so that it would burn until the morning. One such night, when he had finished his supper, the miller's wife said to him :

' Robert, do you have to go back to the mill tonight ? You have worked hard all day.'

' I must, my dear,' replied her husband ; ' if I do not tend the fire the corn will not keep dry, and I shall not be able to grind it into flour, nor sell the flour to the bakers to get money to buy more food for you to make me another excellent supper like the one I have just eaten.'

Off the miller went, down the neat little path of the neat little garden, through the small wooden gate and across to his mill. There he stoked up the fire and, having done this, decided he must wash his grimy hands. He filled a round bowl of water and placed it on a table. Then he remembered he had no towel in the mill with which to dry his hands. Leaving the bowl where it was, full of warm clean water, he returned to his house.

In those days water had to be drawn in a bucket from a well, so it was more precious than it is to us nowadays when all we have to do is to turn on a tap, and the miller, having asked his wife for a towel, felt it better to return to the mill and use his bowl of water than draw more at the well and wash his hands in the house.

Once again he made a journey to the mill. It was now some time after midnight. He climbed up the long wooden steps that led into the main room of the mill, and quietly opened the door.

He glanced at the table where his bowl of water stood, then he rubbed his eyes. Surely he must be dreaming ! But no, there, in the bowl of water, two very small people were bathing ; they were so small that the miller wondered for a moment how they could possibly have reached the table. There was a chair at the side, and he soon realised they must have climbed up with the aid of this. The little people were laughing and chatting and obviously very much enjoying their bath. They had not seen the miller and he, not wishing to disturb them, left his mill and hurried back to his wife to tell her the amazing news.

' Mary, what do you think ? ' he said breathlessly. ' There are two tiny people taking a bath in the bowl of water I left in the mill. Who, and what, can they be ? '

THE MILLER AND THE FAIRIES

The miller would not have been surprised if his wife had accused him of dreaming, but Mary did no such thing.

'You didn't disturb them, Robert, did you?' she asked.

The miller shook his head.

'That's good, for the little folk must be fairies, and it is bad to annoy the fairies. On the other hand, if they are pleased, there is no knowing what reward we may reap.'

'Fairies!' exclaimed the miller, 'fairies! Well, fancy that! Just wait and see what the neighbours will say when I tell them I have had fairies bathing in my mill.'

'No, you must tell no-one about this, my dear,' said his wife. 'The fairies like such things to be kept secret and will not come again if you speak about it to other people.'

The next morning when the miller went to his mill, he found that the fairies had left the place clean and tidy. It must have taken them a long time for mills are big and dusty places, which is perhaps why people whose name is Miller are sometimes nick-named 'Dusty'. Not only had the fairies cleaned and tidied but, on the table at the side of the bowl, they had left a pile of golden coins.

'Such generosity!' said the miller as he showed the money to his wife.

'When the fairies are grateful, they are always generous,' replied his wife. 'You must leave another bowl of water for them to bath in tonight.'

Every night the miller left the bowl of water for the fairies, but now he put it on the floor so they would have no difficulty in reaching it. Sometimes when the miller returned quietly after midnight and peeped through the door, he would find that the two fairies he had first seen were joined by many others, as small and as dainty, all laughing and splashing each other and thoroughly enjoying themselves. And every morning the miller found his mill clean and tidy, and every morning, at the side of the bowl, would be stacked the pile of golden coins.

Soon it became obvious to their neighbours that the miller and his wife were flourishing. They bought more food, dressed in finer clothes and even owned a little brown pony and a yellow trap. The miller found it more and more difficult not to tell his neighbours about his good fortune, and one day he could keep quiet no longer. A friend stopped him in the road and, admiring the miller's new coat and silk-embroidered waistcoat, laughingly said :

' Folk round here are saying you must have taken to crime, Robert, so fine are the clothes you and your good wife are now able to afford.'

The miller flushed angrily for he was an honest man and did not like the suggestion that he might be a criminal.

' No, no ! ' he shouted, ' that is not true. We buy our clothes with the fairy money.'

' Fairy money ? ' asked his friend. ' What do you mean ? '

Before he could stop himself, the miller had told him about the fairies bathing in his mill and the gold they left in payment.

When he reached the little house the miller, somewhat ashamed of himself for revealing their secret, confessed to his wife what he had done. How she scolded him !

' You foolish man,' she said ; ' oh, dear, was there ever such a foolish man ? '

' I daresay the fairies won't find out that I have talked about them,' said the miller. ' Certainly I didn't see any little folk while I was speaking to my friend.'

' That does not mean to say the fairies did not see you, you great idiot,' replied his wife, ' but I don't suppose *you* will ever see them again.'

The miller's wife was right. After midnight the miller went hopefully to his mill and peeped through the door. There on the floor lay the bowl of water he had left for them but there was no sign of the fairies.

In the morning the bowl was still there, the water clean and unused. The mill was dusty and untidy just as the miller had left it, and by the side of the bowl he did not see the pile of golden coins.

Never again did the fairies take a bath in the mill, never again did they clean and tidy the mill, and never again did they leave their gift of money. In return for their help and friendship, the fairies like to have their deeds kept very secret indeed.

Dewi Dal ﷼

DEWI DAL was an unhappy man. He was a farmer and, as he had to get up early and very often could not get to bed until late, he needed his few hours' sleep. And he was not managing to get this. There was too much noise at night. And he didn't know what he could do about it because the noise was made by the fairies. Dewi Dal's home was overrun with fairies. They caused no trouble at all during the day but at night they laughed and sang, rushed up and down the stairs, turned the rooms upside down, ate the food, broke the china and generally behaved very badly. The house rang with the chatter of their voices and the clatter of their tiny feet.

At last Dewi Dal was unable to bear it any longer ; he had not slept for weeks, his face was pale and haggard, there were black circles under his eyes and his work on the farm was suffering because he felt too tired to do it. So he went to consult a wise man about his problem.

'I don't want to anger the fairy folk,' he explained, 'and indeed if they would only be quiet, I could put up with their pranks. Is there any way I can get rid of them without annoying them ?'

The wise man said he thought there was and gave Dewi Dal some instructions to carry out the next day.

It so happened it was time to cut the corn in the Cae Mawr, which means the Big Field, and this was a day's work for fifteen men.

Dewi Dal's home was overrun with fairies

Dewi Dal had told his wife what the wise man had said, and instructed her in the part she was to play. In the morning, at breakfast time, she said loud enough for the fairies, wherever they might be hidden, to hear :

' Dewi, I will prepare the food for the fifteen men who are going to reap the Cae Mawr.'

' Yes, do, my dear,' replied Dewi Dal in an equally loud voice, ' and make sure the food is filling and sufficient.'

' They shall be fed according to our means,' his wife assured him.

She then set about the preparation of the meal. She caught a tiny sparrow in the garden, plucked it of its feathers, trussed it and roasted it, as she would have done a chicken, on a spit before the kitchen fire. Then she poured some salt into a nutshell, cut a small square of thin bread and placed these on the table, together with the roast sparrow, ready for the fifteen reapers.

The fairies, who had been watching her from their secret hiding-places, were amazed to see the size of the meal that had been prepared for fifteen hefty, hungry men.

' Can this meagre meal be meant for grown men ? ' whispered one fairy.

' It looks as if it must be,' said another.

' Did you not hear her say they should be fed according to Dewi Dal's means ? ' asked a third.

' If they are so poor as to serve one sparrow for fifteen men,' said a fourth, ' we must leave this place at once. There is nothing left for us here.'

The farmer's wife heard the whispering and when this was followed by a scampering of tiny feet, as if an army of mice were on the retreat, she knew the wise man's plan had worked, and she laughed softly to herself.

That night Dewi Dal and his family had the first good night's rest they had had for a very long time.

Nefyn the Mermaid ✺

IFAN MORGAN was a poor fisherman who lived in a village
on the coast of Caernarvonshire. One day he was wandering
along the deserted beach in search of driftwood to burn on his
little cottage fire, when it began to rain heavily. He had little
protection and began to look for somewhere to shelter. He
noticed a narrow opening amongst the rocks near the cliff-side
and, squeezing through this, he made his way into a cave where
the darkness temporarily prevented him from seeing anything,
and where the only sound he could hear was the drip drip of
the water running down the walls and the squelch of the seaweed
under his feet.

He had not gone far into the cave when he heard a loud squeal
and, his eyes now accustomed to the dark, he saw in front of him,
lying stretched out on a rocky ledge, her tail towards him, a
beautiful and naked mermaid. She continued to scream at the
sight of him.

'Please be quiet,' coaxed Ifan, 'I'm not going to hurt you,
and you really are making a terrible noise.'

As a matter of fact, the noise reminded him of the cries of the
great grey seals that could sometimes be seen on the seashore.

The mermaid was soon quiet, and Ifan talked to her gently
until at last she spoke to him and told him that her name was
Nefyn.

'Do not stay here any longer,' she begged him.

' Do you not like me, then ? ' asked Ifan.

' Yes, yes, I do, and that is why I want you to go. My brother will be coming soon and might not be pleased to find you here. Please, please, go now, and come back to meet me here tomorrow.'

Ifan agreed to do this, and made his way out of the cave. But when he had squeezed through its narrow entrance, he found the sea had come in and he could go no farther. A huge wave dashed against the rocks, caught up Ifan and dragged him out to sea, but luckily the tide was still coming in and another wave carried him farther up the beach and threw him on to the shore.

He staggered to his feet, and found that while he had been in the sea a rope had wound itself around his waist, the end of which was still dangling in the water. He unwound it and, as it was a fine strong piece of rope, he began to haul it in. This was harder work than Ifan expected it to be ; it was as if there were something attached to the other end of it. And indeed as Ifan pulled it in, he also hauled ashore a coffer which, when opened, he found was full of treasure. He spent the night carrying this treasure home and, as he made the journeys to and fro, he puzzled about his good fortune, and came to the conclusion that the coffer was a present from the lovely mermaid he had met in the cave.

The following day he went back to the cave to thank her, but he was late and Nefyn was nowhere to be seen.

Sad at heart, he went home and to bed where, having had little rest the night before, he soon fell fast asleep. He was roused by the sound of Nefyn's voice. She was peeping in through his cottage window.

' Ifan,' she called, ' come to see me in the cave tomorrow, and do not be late this time.'

Before he could reply, she had disappeared ; and next morning he wondered if he had dreamt it all. However, he was taking no chances and he set off for the cave in good time. There he found Nefyn sitting on the same rocky ledge, combing her long wet hair with a mother-of-pearl comb ; but she was no longer naked and her form was human.

'You have lost your fish-tail !' exclaimed Ifan a little rudely.

'I am come to live now on the land like you,' she replied, 'though I am the daughter of a sea king. See, here is my crown,' and Nefyn placed on her head a circlet of pure gold, 'and here is a cap for you.'

Nefyn held out a cap of beautiful workmanship and Ifan put it on his head, proud to have such a present from a princess.

'I have long loved you, Ifan,' the mermaid confessed. 'I have often seen you glide through our waters in your father's white boat. I first fell in love with your voice. Once I heard you sing a song that I tried to repeat at my father's court but I never could, and I never heard you sing it again. My family gave me permission to come here with my treasures and learn the song from you.'

'I will teach you gladly,' said Ifan, 'if you will marry me.'

Nefyn consented to be his wife, and soon they were married in the little village church. They lived happily together for many years ; they had ten children, five sets of twins, a boy and a girl each time.

The treasure that Nefyn had brought with her from the sea lay hidden still in the cave, but every now and again she and her husband secretly went there to collect some of it, and in this way they were able to live comfortably.

The children were not told of their mother's secret and not

one of them knew that she had once been a mermaid. One day, however, they began to have their suspicions.

The family were out on the sea in a boat, enjoying themselves, when a great storm arose. The youngest children clung fearfully to their mother while the older ones tried to help their father steer the boat through the wild black waters. Above the noise of the storm could be heard unearthly wailings which Nefyn knew came from her father's kingdom but which further terrified her family.

Presently she bent over the side of the boat and murmured something to the sea that the children could not hear. Instantly the storm abated and all was calm. Nefyn refused to answer her children's questions, and they remained bewildered about her unusual influence over the sea.

Not long after this some of the older children were in the village street when they passed a group of ill-natured women who started to laugh at them. One child began to cry, and the eldest boy, whose name was Nefyd, turned on the women and demanded :

' Why do you laugh at us, old women ? '

' Because you are offspring of a strange mother,' jeered one woman.

' What do you mean by that ? ' asked Nefyd.

' Your mother was a mermaid, didn't you know ? ' chanted another spiteful woman.

The children turned away, most of them not caring if this were the truth or not, but the eldest boy was very upset. He recalled the strange ways of his mother, the long journeys she made with his father and the strange lands she sometimes talked about.

One night he overheard Ifan tell the servants that he and his wife would be going away for a long time. Quietly Nefyd

NEFYN THE MERMAID

followed his parents when they left the house. Down the
village street they walked, across the fields, down the cliff path,
and on to the beach that gleamed long and white in the moonlight.

The boy hid behind a rock and watched Ifan and Nefyn walk
towards the edge of the sea. There Nefyn put a leather mantle
round herself and her husband and, as a wave crashed on to the
shore, they threw themselves into it and disappeared. Their son
then knew that his mother was a mermaid and that he had just
seen his parents off on one of their many journeys to Nefyn's
home under the sea.

Broken-hearted at this discovery, he went home and, in nine
days' time, he was dead from shock. This left the second son,
Tegid, in charge. Now Tegid was afraid of nothing, neither
was he ashamed to know that his mother came from sea-fairy folk.

'Take my brother's body to the seashore,' he ordered the
servants, 'that my mother's people may fetch him for burial.'

The funeral party wove its melancholy way down to the shore.
The brothers and sisters waited by the coffin until it was midnight.
Then, out of the sea, appeared a merman clad in armour like the
silver scales of a fish.

'Bring the boy's coffin to the water,' he ordered, 'he is to be
united with his mother's people, and shall have a heart that no
weight can break.'

The coffin was dragged to the water's edge and, as soon as
the first wave had touched it, Nefyd leapt out of the box, and
was seen by his brothers and sisters walking across the water
with the merman towards a ship that waited for them out at
sea. As the fairy ship sailed away, gliding magically over billows
that it scarcely touched, the family on the shore could hear the
strains of enchanting music. They returned home quietly, glad
that their brother was going to a land where he would be happy.

A year later Ifan returned, but without Nefyn. He went to bed on the night of his return, and the next morning he was dead. On the day of his funeral his wife appeared, and her distress was so great that she bade goodbye to her children, saying :

' I am going back to your grandfather's kingdom beneath the sea ; now that your dear father is dead, I no longer wish to live here.'

And she was never more seen on dry land.

Tegid again took charge of the family, and proved to be a fine man of high principles and great generosity. Only once were he and his brothers ever to be reminded that they had sea-fairy blood in their veins, and they were never to forget that occasion for the rest of their lives.

They were out fishing in a nearby bay when a fierce wind blew up. No storm accompanied it but, battle hard as the brothers might, they were unable to prevent their boat being carried off far out to sea. When the wind died down they found they were in the most wonderful spot they had ever seen. The sea was still and smooth as glass and, looking into it, the brothers could see, not far away, a lovely country of bright green fields and soft green valleys, hedges of gaily coloured flowers, groves of slender trees that waved like sea-weed in the water, and rivers winding lazily through the countryside, past mansions of unbelievable beauty. Looking again, they could see the people of this land, their mother's land, enjoying themselves in song and dance, and the gentle waves that now began to move on the surface of the sea, blotting out the merry picture, gave out a faint echo of the sweet music as they rippled to and fro. The brothers rowed for home and the enchanting music charmed their ears until they reached the shore.

The Farmer and the Fairy Cow ✺

IN a lake in the hills, not far from Aberdovey, there lived some lake fairies, lovely ladies who wore long green dresses that were the colour of the cool water underneath which they lived.

Every evening these fairies would appear at the edge of the lake with their milk-white hounds and their herd of milk-white cows. These cows would graze on the lush pasture around the lake while their fairy owners chatted and danced and sang close beside them. The cows, dogs and fairies were quite a familiar sight to the human people who lived near by, and no-one dared to go near them when they appeared in the evenings. But one day one of the fairy cows, unseen by its fairy owners, strayed away and joined the herd of a human farmer called Idris whose land bordered one side of the lake. The fairies returned as usual that evening to their home beneath the water, taking with them their dogs and their herd of cows, but the one that had strayed remained behind.

When Idris arrived to herd his grazing cows back to the farm, he immediately noticed among them this magnificent milk-white cow.

'Oh !' he exclaimed with excitement, 'it is one of the fairy cows. If it will only stay with me, what a lucky man I shall be.'

Well, it did stay, and it appeared to be quite happy among its more ordinary brothers and sisters. But the happiness of the fairy cow was nothing compared to the happiness of Farmer

Idris ; no other farmer had ever possessed such a cow. The milk that it gave was rich and foamy, and the cow yielded each day as much of this milk as a whole herd of mortal cows would do in a week. The butter was golden and delicious, such butter had never been tasted before in the county. The cheese, too, had so fine a flavour it might well have come from paradise. And as for the cream, it was so wonderful that people came from miles around to buy it. Indeed people came from miles around to buy all the produce of what was now known as ' Idris's fairy cow '.

Idris had always been a poor farmer. His land was not fertile, his farm animals had never been successful, and work as he often did from dawn until after dusk, he had never managed to make more than a bare living from his farm. After the arrival of the fairy cow, things began to change for him. Before long he was a very rich man. The fairy cow had calves and when those calves became cows they had calves, so that Idris now had a vast herd of cattle all with some fairy blood in them, and all of them producing wonderful milk like the first fairy cow.

All would have gone well if only Idris had been satisfied with his good fortune, but unhappily he was a greedy man, and when he saw that the first fairy cow was getting old and no longer able to give him more calves or more milk, he was dissatisfied.

' That cow is getting old,' he said to his wife, ' and is no longer any use to me. I think I'll fatten her up for the butcher. Her meat ought to fetch a good price.'

' It seems a pity,' replied his wife. ' She has been a good cow to you. Could you not let her live in peace now she is old ? She deserves better treatment than being sent to the butcher.'

But Idris would not listen to his wife. He began to feed the fairy cow with plenty of rich food so that soon she was enormous ;

in fact she was the fattest cow he had ever seen, and every day she became fatter until it looked as if she might burst.

The day came when, Idris having decided she could certainly never be any fatter than she was, the butcher was sent for to kill her. Idris's neighbours were invited to the killing and, together with the farmer and his wife, they watched the butcher, with his blue and white apron tied round his thick waist and his huge axe in one hand, climb up the hill towards the farm. The cow was led out of her stall into the yard.

' How fat she is, how fat ! ' cried the crowd with admiration.

The butcher reached the yard and stared at the cow.

' How fat she is, how fat ! ' he said with astonishment.

Everything was now ready for the fatal blow to be struck. Idris and his neighbours waited expectantly. Idris's wife shivered a little ; she felt sorry for the lovely old milk-white fairy cow, and somehow she was sure no good would come of this killing.

The butcher raised high the axe, ready to strike the blow but, before he could lower it, the air was filled with a terrible cry. The axe fell to the ground without having touched the cow. Everyone looked towards the lake from whence the cry came, and there they saw, standing on a crag in the middle of the lake, one of the lovely lake fairies, dressed in her frock of green, her arms beckoning towards them.

' Come, fairy cow,' shouted the fairy in a voice of thunder, ' come, fairy cow, come home, come home.'

The fairy cow had lifted its head and was listening intently. As soon as the fairy's voice reached her and before anyone could realise exactly what was happening, the cow had run towards the lake and after her pounded her children and her grandchildren and her great-grandchildren. Above the clattering roar their hooves made upon the dry earth, the fairy's voice could still be heard urging them to 'Come, fairy cows, come, fairy cows, come home, come home.'

'After them,' shouted Idris desperately as he saw all his wealth, together with his whole herd of fairy cows, rushing towards the lake. And after them ran, as fast as their legs would carry them, Idris and his neighbours. But they reached the edge of the lake only just in time to see the fairy herd plunge into it. Silently they watched the fairy and the milk-white cows disappear beneath the cool water. Only one sign remained to show that the cows had ever existed. Where each one had vanished in the water appeared a beautiful white water-lily and the whole lake was ever afterwards covered with this carpet of snowy blossoms.

Idris lived to regret his greed for he never prospered again, and soon he was as poor a farmer as he had been before the day when the milk-white cow had strayed from her fairy home.

The Disappearance of Ifan Gruffydd's Daughter

M ANY years ago there lived a man in Anglesey called Ifan
Gruffydd. He was a poor man but he had two precious
possessions which he would not have exchanged for a barrel of
gold or a prince's palace.

The most precious of these two things was his sweet and
lovely daughter Olwen, and his other prized possession was a
brindle cow that yielded rich milk, and of whom Ifan was so
fond she seemed almost like one of the family.

One morning when Olwen went out to the cow byre to
milk the cow, she found it empty.

'Father,' called out Olwen, 'I cannot find the cow; she
must have strayed.'

Ifan immediately came running out of the cottage and he,
too, was unable to find the cow anywhere near at hand.

'We must search the country for her,' he told his daughter,
'for I cannot afford to lose her, and indeed should be most
distressed were anything to happen to her. She is a good cow.'

So Olwen fetched her shawl, and the two of them went off
to search for the lost beast. Up and down the whole neighbourhood they went, asking all their neighbours if the cow had been
seen in their direction. But they had no luck, and the cows they
saw in the fields were all those belonging to other people, and
not one of them had the handsome appearance of Ifan Gruffydd's
brindle cow.

All day father and daughter searched until at last Ifan said :

' It's no good, Olwen, it will soon be dark. We must give up and go home.'

' Perhaps we shall find her tomorrow, Father dear,' comforted Olwen.

On their way home they had to cross a field and, when they were half-way across it, Ifan clutched Olwen's arm and whispered :

' Look, look, over there ! What do you see ? '

' Surely not the cow ! ' exclaimed Olwen, peering ahead of her into the dusk.

' No, no, I would that it were,' replied her father, ' but it's something very strange.'

Olwen followed her father's pointing finger with her eyes until she could just see a ring of little moving figures, small men galloping around in a circle on ponies even tinier than the small Welsh mountain pony.

' Who can they be, Father ? ' asked Olwen.

' Fairy folk,' her father told her. ' Let us move a little closer where we may see them more clearly.'

Quietly they both crept forward through the long grass until Ifan stopped and said :

' This is near enough ; it might be dangerous to go farther.'

But Olwen was eager to see the little riders more closely and, not heeding her father's advice, she crept on until, without realising it, she was actually within the circle where the midget ponies galloped. And at that moment she was lost to her father's sight, and so were the fairy men.

Forgotten now was Ifan's worry about his lost cow, his lost daughter was far more important. Frantically he searched for her up and down the large field but it was no use, she was nowhere to be found and, after some hours, he was forced to go home without her.   When he reached home he found the brindle cow had returned to the byre of her own accord, but Ifan was too worried now about Olwen to feel much pleasure about the cow's return.

A few days later, as Olwen still had not been found, Ifan Gruffydd went to see a friend of his called John Roberts who had the reputation of being a very wise man and something of a magician into the bargain.   Ifan told his friend what had happened to Olwen and asked for his advice.

'Don't worry, Ifan,' said John Roberts, 'if you do what I tell you, you will see your daughter again, but you must have patience.   In a year's time at the anniversary of the very hour of the night when you lost Olwen you must return to the spot, taking with you four of your strongest friends.'

John Roberts went on to tell Ifan why he would need the friends, and exactly what he was to do when they reached the field in a year's time.   And this is what happened.

The year went slowly for Ifan Gruffydd—he was lonely and sad without Olwen—but at last the day came for her to be rescued from the fairies.

With four stalwart friends he set off in the evening for the field where he had last seen his daughter.   The five men crouched down in the grass and stayed there, silent and unmoving, for an hour or so ; then they heard the noise of tiny hooves and, looking across the field, they saw the little men galloping their ponies round and round the fairy ring—and amongst them was Olwen, riding round with them on a pony of her own.

Remembering the advice of John Roberts, Ifan tied a strong rope round his waist and gave the end of it to his friends to hold.   Then he crept up to the fairy circle, quickly darted into it and, pulling his daughter off the pony, he held her firmly in his arms. His friends, on a sign from him, began to tug and, although the magic of the fairy ring was very strong, the four men proved stronger, and managed to drag Olwen and her father out of it to safety.

'Oh, Olwen,' sighed her father with relief, and embracing her warmly, 'how good it is to have you back with me again !'

Olwen gazed at him in surprise.

'Father, what an odd thing to say ! Anyone would think we had been parted for a long time. Come on, let's go home and, as I said before, we will look for the cow again tomorrow.'

'The cow was found a year ago,' her father said, 'on the night that you joined the fairy riders.'

But it was difficult to convince Olwen of this ; such is the magic of fairy time, she thought she had only been with the little men for a few minutes.

John the Painter ✍️

THERE was a certain John Davies who had once been a
carpenter but, as he had not excelled at this job, had decided
to turn painter. We are not told if he was a good painter but
we do know he was a very fine musician, especially on the flute,
which he always carried with him wherever he went.

One October he was returning home from Aberayron over
the high lands of Cardiganshire and, anxious not to be too late,
he stopped only for a moment at one inn to quench his thirst
and to give him courage to meet any ghosts or fairies he might
come across on his last three miles.

When he left the inn darkness had fallen ; there was no
moon and the clouds in the sky had hidden the friendly stars,
so John had to walk along slowly over the moor, guided only
by the hawthorn hedge that edged the road. It was with relief
that he soon saw a bright light ahead of him.

' Ah,' said John to himself, ' that must be a light from old
Peggi's cottage, so now I know where I am.'

He went in the direction of the light but, instead of burning
brightly in one spot, it began to move and jump about so that
John became suspicious. To make matters worse, he had been
so bent on following the light that he had strayed off the road
and now was lost on the moor. But the moving light was
brighter and nearer ; on a sudden, John found himself near
a fairy ring where a great number of exquisite little fairy

ladies were dancing in white dresses that only reached their knees.

Before he had had time to get over his surprise, one of these fairies took him by the arm.

'Come,' she said firmly, 'let us dance together,' and soon John found himself caught up with the whirling dancers, and he was overjoyed to find that his clumsy feet seemed to have gained a new lightness and grace. He would never have forgiven himself had he trodden on the lovely and delicate toes of his fairy partner.

For a long time they danced together until at last John was almost too tired to go on. His dancing partner was as fresh as ever, and might have insisted on continuing with the dance had not the Queen appeared. The Fairy Queen stood, little gold crown twinkling on her fairy brow and her straight black hair falling like a cloak about her shoulders, and she lifted one smooth milk-white arm and beckoned imperiously to John who willingly stopped dancing and went over to her.

'Who are you, mortal man?' demanded the Queen haughtily, 'and where do you come from?'

'I come from a village not far from here, madam,' replied John respectfully, bowing low to the little Queen, 'and I am a painter by trade.'

The Queen appeared quite disinterested in this fact, dismissing it with a curt, 'Fairies have no need of painters.'

But John was not to be dismissed so easily from the royal presence.

'I am a musician, too, madam,' he said proudly.

The Fairy Queen's face brightened at this and, with a wave of the hand, she bade her fairy subjects to stop dancing for a moment.

'That is better news,' she said. 'You may entertain us with your music. Have you an instrument?'

John said he had and, producing his flute from his coat pocket, he began to play a variety of airs. The Queen and her fairies listened but as he went from one tune to another, there was little sign of pleasure on their faces even though John played the flute so well. Indeed, they began to murmur angrily amongst themselves.

The fairy with whom John had danced leant over and whispered in his ear:

'They are cross with you, you know.'

'But why?' asked John. 'I play my flute well, don't I?'

'Yes, indeed you do, but these tunes you play are Irish, Scottish and English airs. We are Welsh fairies. Do you not know any Welsh airs?'

Smiling gratefully at the helpful fairy, John immediately began to play a well-known Welsh tune and the frowns of the beautiful little ladies gradually changed to smiles and nods of approval.

On went John from one Welsh air to another. Soon some of the fairies were dancing again, others were singing to his music in their high sweet voices, while the Queen herself gaily tapped her foot to the merry rhythm.

Certainly John was beginning to make a better impression on her than he had done at first, but he nearly spoilt everything for himself. He was a little tired and a little thirsty, so he put down his flute and asked if he might have a glass of beer.

'Mortal man,' said the Queen sternly, 'that request ill becomes you. Do you not know that fairies never touch alcohol of any sort?'

John bowed his head in shame, and accepted a bowl of cold

On went John from one Welsh air to another

river water instead. Then, to regain the Queen's favour, he recommenced the playing of his flute.

While he was playing he had time to notice the special beauty and grace of the fairy with whom he had danced, and who had been kind to him. This fairy smiled at him so bewitchingly every time he looked at her that John found himself very much in love.

The Queen seemed in a better mood, so once again he approached her.

'Have you enjoyed my music, madam?' he inquired.

The Queen graciously inclined her head.

'Then,' continued John, 'may I have one of your lovely fairies as my bride for I must confess I am deeply in love with her'—and he pointed at his dancing partner.

The Queen appeared uncertain about giving her permission, so John further pressed his suit.

'I have a horse at home called Bob,' he said nervously,

although one might wonder of what great advantage this would be either to him or a fairy wife.

Still the Queen said nothing.

'And a cart I made myself,' added the suitor quickly.

One can imagine that if John had had to give up carpentry for painting, the cart he made himself was not likely to have been up to much, and no doubt the Queen realised this for she remained unimpressed.

'However,' she told him, 'there can be little doubt as to your ability as a musician and for that alone I consent to your request.'

John's joy was unbounded, and the fairy of his choice came to him and took his hand in hers to show that she, too, was pleased.

'I give her to you on one condition,' said the Queen, 'that you and your future wife visit us here once a month when the moon is full.'

John agreed, and the Queen turned to one of her ladies, whispered a few words and then took from her a roughly shaped pot full to the brim with glittering gold. This she held out to John, saying :

'This is the fairy dowry that comes to you with your fairy bride.'

John put out his hands to take the treasure but that was the nearest he was ever to get to it for at that moment there came an interruption. And this was the way of it.

Old Peggi, whose cottage light John thought he had seen before he came across the fairies, was awakened early in the morning by the sound of music. This puzzled her as she had no near neighbours and, anyway, it was a curious time of the day for folk to be making merry. She rose, dressed herself and went outside where she saw John, sitting on the grass, seemingly alone, and blowing into a flute.

' What are you doing here ? ' shouted the old woman, shaking him hard by the shoulder.

The fairies, whom only John could see, instantly disappeared at sight and sound of old Peggi, taking with them the crock of gold and John's bride-to-be.

Peggi was faced with a scowling man who looked as if he had just awoken from a long, deep dream, and she was never to understand to her dying day why he shook his fist at her and angrily exclaimed :

' Oh, you stupid old woman, you have just ruined everything for me. I was making the best bargain of my life and through your silly interference I have lost two most precious treasures ! '

Old Peggi went off hurriedly, muttering to herself, and left John alone with his flute. ' Surely,' the old woman told herself, ' as it is too early for that John Davies to be drunk, he must indeed be mad ! '

The Fairy Garden ≈◑

IN the mountains of Breconshire there was once a small lake, and near this lake was a great rock, and in the great rock there was a tiny door. The door was open only one day in the year, and that was on a certain day in May. Anyone who wished to go through the door on this day was welcome to do so. The visitor had to go down a secret passage which ended in an island in the centre of the lake. On this island was the most exquisite garden it is possible to imagine. The flowers were of gorgeous colours and rare variety, the fruit hung luscious, ripe and ready to pick from the trees, and the grass was so bright it could only be described as fairy green. As a matter of fact the grass was indeed fairy grass : this enchanting place was the home of fairies.

Those who stood on the edge of the lake could scarcely see the island, which could only be reached through the rock door, but occasionally strains of music were wafted to the shore.

Guests who visited on the special day in May were always made welcome by the fairies and enjoyed themselves greatly, being given as much fruit as they could eat and as many flowers as they could carry or decorate themselves with. But their fairy hosts made one condition : none of these gifts was to be taken away.

Unfortunately an occasion arose when the fairy island was visited by a greedy wretch who disobeyed fairy instructions, and this is never a wise thing to do. This man was tempted to take home with him a magnificent scarlet flower that had been given to him ; he slipped the blossom into his pocket and crept away down the secret passage before it was really time to leave. When he opened the door in the rock and stepped out on to human land again, he suddenly felt giddy and collapsed unconscious on the ground. He did not recover until some time later, and then he found the fairy flower had vanished from his pocket.

The fairies, of course, knew what he had done and although they bade farewell courteously to their other guests when it was time for them to leave, they closed the door that night for ever. Thus did one man's foolishness deprive many people of their yearly pleasure.

Undoubtedly the fairies still play and sing and work in their lovely hidden garden somewhere in Breconshire. The lake can probably still be found, but the door in the rock has not been opened again, and it is doubtful if it can ever be seen by the human eye.

The Flooding of the Lower Hundred ✌➣

WHERE now lie the waters of Cardigan Bay was once a fair and prosperous land called Cantr'r Gwaelod or the Lower Hundred, and it was through the neglect of one man that this land exists no longer.

The Lower Hundred was ruled by a man called Gwyddno who, because he was tall, was nicknamed Gwyddno Garanhir, Gwyddno the Long-Legged. As the country was low-lying— it was actually below the level of the sea—it was protected by a great dyke such as those that protect the lowlands of Holland to this day. The gates of this dyke were opened when the tide was going out to allow the river water to flow away, and closed when the tide was coming in to protect the land from flooding.

It was a great honour to be appointed keeper of the dyke gates, and the last man to be appointed was Seithenyn, son of the King of Dyfed. Next to Gwyddno, Seithenyn was the most important man in the Lower Hundred, and both he and his lord were fond of giving banquets.

One night Gwyddno held a banquet in his palace. The feasting and the revelry were at their height when the harpist, who was accompanying the singing and dancing, suddenly stopped playing. Raising his eyes from his harp, he gazed in terror across the long hall ; then, in a ringing voice, he cried out :

'Doom is upon us ! Doom is upon us ! We must flee for our lives.'

A shiver ran through the company and the noise of their chatter and laughter died down. No-one moved except Gwyddno who, striding up to the harpist, demanded of him :

' What do you mean by frightening my people in this unseemly manner ? '

' Doom is upon us ! ' repeated the harpist in a dazed voice. ' The flood is upon us.'

' Nonsense,' said Gwyddno firmly, ' how can the flood be upon us when the noble Seithenyn is guarding the dyke gates ? '

The harpist said nothing but turned his head towards the banqueting-table at the end of the hall ; then he lifted his hand and pointed in the same direction. Hundreds of eyes followed his finger but Gwyddno was the first to see at what it pointed.

There, lying under the table in a drunken stupor, was Seithenyn who should at that moment have been shutting the dyke gates to keep out the incoming tide.

Panic broke out as the people realised what had happened. Tables and chairs were overturned, tapestries were torn down and the smallest and weakest men and women were trampled underfoot as the crowd rushed for the doors. Above the noise of the terrified people inside the palace could be heard the wailing of those outside, who had already seen the steady flow of water begin to drown their homes and country.

A great wind arose, adding its screaming voice to the tumult and whipping up the water into huge wild waves that tore their way inland, carrying all before them. When at last the wind died down, the sea had already silenced every other noise, and the land and many of the people of the Lower Hundred had disappeared altogether.

Now Gwyddno and some of his followers had managed to remain calm and they, together with the harpist, had saddled

132

their fastest horses and, not waiting to rescue any of their possessions, had ridden swiftly away to the north where lay the
safe and high ground of Snowdonia.

At dawn the next day, Gwyddno stood on a high peak and
gazed down upon the now sea-washed land over which he had
once reigned. He uttered no word of condemnation of Seithenyn,
who had been too drunk to escape drowning. He uttered no
word at all, he just let out a long and enormous sigh, and perhaps
if you should ever find the spot where Gwyddno stood and were
to listen carefully, you would still hear the echo of that solitary
sigh, ' the sigh of Gwyddno the Long-Legged when the wave
rolled over his land ' as a Welsh proverb says to this day.

But Gwyddno was not the man to spend the rest of his life
bemoaning his unhappy lot. He had lost everything, so he
settled in a fishing-village near Aberystwyth and also near the
sea that had once been the Land of the Lower Hundred, and
there he made his living out of fish.

Fate dealt kindly with him ; not only did he have a valuable
fishery, he also owned a remarkable basket ; if food enough for
one man was put into this, when it was next opened that same
food would have turned into enough for a hundred men. Thus
Gwyddno prospered, although he did not forget until his dying
day that dreadful night when Seithenyn neglected his duty with
such far-reaching and dire results.

The Hound Gelert ॐ

PRINCE LLEWELLYN, Prince of Wales, was a great hunts-
man, and when he married the daughter of King John of
England his father-in-law gave him a beautiful hound as a
wedding-present. The name of the hound was Gelert.

Not only was Gelert a fine hunting-dog, he was also a good-
natured animal who soon endeared himself to Llewellyn and his
family. In fact he was their favourite dog, and some huntsmen
said that he was petted too much inside the castle for him to be
of much use for hunting outside it. But Prince Llewellyn knew
that this was not so.

One day the Prince decided he would like a day's sport and,
gathering dogs and huntsmen together, he was about to set out
on his horse when he noticed that Gelert was missing. He ordered
the hunting-horn to be sounded again, but still Gelert did not
appear. This was a disappointment to the Prince for, in spite of
what some of the huntsmen said, he knew Gelert to be his best
hound, and he was sure the day's hunting would not be a complete
success without him. However, time was getting on and, reluctantly, he led the hunt away and left Gelert, he knew not where,
behind him.

Now Gelert was actually inside the castle, lying at the side of
Llewellyn's baby son, who was asleep in his cradle. He heard
the hunting-horn and raised his head for a moment. He would
dearly have loved to go hunting on that fine winter's morning,

134

but nonetheless he did not move ; if he went, who would take care of the child ? The womenfolk were busy with their house-work in another part of the castle, and the baby's mother was at her prayers in the chapel. So he lowered his head again and lay with it between his paws, his soft brown eyes never leaving the cradle.

It was perhaps half an hour later that Gelert heard an un-familiar sound. He pricked up his ears and sniffed the air. Something or someone was shuffling slowly up the deserted corridor outside, whose scent Gelert did not recognise. He rose to his feet and placed himself protectively in front of the cradle. The half-shut door moved a little and into the room, head lowered and fangs showing, walked a great ugly brute of a wolf, twice as big as Gelert, yet lean and obviously hungry. It had been a hard winter and the wolves had become very bold in their search for food.

For a second Gelert and the wolf stared at each other, then the wolf looked beyond Gelert and saw the baby ; deciding that here indeed was a tasty meal for him, he leapt towards the cradle. But Gelert leapt too, straight for the wolf's throat, and the two of them were locked together, snarling and biting, the great strength of the hungry wolf pitted against the lesser strength of the better-fed Gelert. In the long and bloody struggle that began between them, the cradle was overturned but the baby lay under it, protected, for the present at any rate.

At last, when it seemed that Gelert had no more strength left, he managed to make one final effort to kill the wolf and, sinking his teeth deep through the harsh grey fur and into the flesh, he succeeded. In a few minutes more he might have been killed himself and the wolf have had his muzzle pushed under the cradle, behind which his huge body now lay. Gelert collapsed on the floor, weak from loss of blood, and began to lick his wounds.

At that moment Prince Llewellyn, having returned early from an unsuccessful hunt, entered the room. And what a terrible sight met his eyes ! Disorder was everywhere, his child's cradle over-turned, pools of blood upon the floor, and the hound Gelert himself covered with blood. Feebly Gelert wagged his tail to greet his master, and unsteadily rose to meet him. But, alas, Llewellyn had jumped to the wrong conclusion.

'Wicked and evil animal,' he thundered, 'you have killed and devoured my only child.'

Gelert's tail dropped between his legs when he heard the anger in his beloved master's voice, and in vain did the brown eyes mutely plead their innocence. Prince Llewellyn drew his sword and plunged it straight through the dog's heart. Gelert died instantly, and his handsome body lay stiff and still at his master's feet. It was then that, for the first time, the baby began to cry. Quickly Llewellyn strode to the cradle and turned it right side up. There lay his bonny son, alive and well and now screaming lustily ; and there, behind the cradle, was the dead body of the biggest wolf Llewellyn had ever seen. At last he realised what had happened, and he was overcome with grief at what he had done. The noble Gelert had saved the life of the Prince's only son and that same Prince, in his hastiness, had rewarded him with death.

The Welsh have a proverb, 'Before revenge, first know the cause,' and it was Prince Llewellyn who first made this saying popular, while the story of him and his brave hound gave rise to another saying, 'As sorry as the man who killed his grey-hound.'

Prince Llewellyn and the Red-Haired Man ✌✚

THERE is another tale told about Prince Llewellyn, and this is it. He was a devout man and loved to spend much time at Trefriw where he would offer up prayers to St Mary of that place. On one occasion he had been praying there before making a journey to see his father-in-law, King John, at his court in London.

He set out for the journey with a hundred of his men, and they had not gone far when they arrived at a place called Cefn Tegeingl. Coming towards them they saw a rough-looking man with red hair, ragged clothes and no shoes. Some of the men began to jeer at him, but the red-haired man took no notice of them and, walking up to Llewellyn's horse, he took hold of the bridle.

' Hey, what d'you think you're doing, eh ? ' shouted one of the Prince's men. ' Take your dirty hands off the bridle of the Prince's horse.'

' Let him be,' said Prince Llewellyn ; ' he does no harm.'

' Where are you going, sire ? ' asked the man.

' Why, to London,' replied the Prince.

' I should like to come with you if you will let me,' said the man, and he seemed so eager the Prince had not the heart to refuse him.

' Come with us, and welcome,' he said.

The red-haired man was given a horse and joined the other

men. Quite soon the Prince forgot about him but, when they reached London and he was dismounting stiffly from his horse, the fellow came up to him again and said :

'Should there be anything you want of me, sire, send for me. I have certain magical powers that could be used to your advantage.'

The Prince thanked him gravely, and they parted. Llewellyn went to King John's court and was made welcome there, although he was but a poor prince, and was not thought of highly in English court circles.

That night there was a banquet, and the King placed Llewellyn at the table of his son, Prince Henry. When the feast was at its end King John's wizard was called for to perform his wonderful feats for the company.

'Now you will see something that nothing in Wales can equal,' whispered Prince Henry to Prince Llewellyn.

The King's wizard was an old man with a long white beard ; he wore magnificent clothes of bright blue brocade that matched his piercing eyes, and decorating his cloak were the various signs of the zodiac in gold and silver. Raising his gnarled hand, he made a few movements in the air, and then it seemed as if the whole banqueting hall was full of the sea with ships sailing on it that carried fine merchandise, and these ships seemed to sail majestically past the astonished eyes of the company. With a wave of his other hand, the wizard caused the sea and the ships to vanish, and in their place appeared a dirty yard about which ran goats, sheep and cattle, while pretty milkmaids milked the cows. The goats even ran along the tables ; one passed right in front of Llewellyn.

'There,' said one of the nobles, 'is this not a remarkable wizard ? I don't suppose you, being a mere prince of Wales, even possess a wizard, let alone one as clever as this.'

PRINCE LLEWELLYN AND THE RED-HAIRED MAN

These words angered Llewellyn, and he called one of his servants to his side.

'Go quickly,' he said, 'and fetch the red-haired man who travelled here with us from Trefriw. Tell him I have need of his services, and here is money that he may arrive dressed in better clothes.'

But when the red-haired man was found, he refused the money for the clothes and arrived at the palace in his rags and barefooted as before.

'With your permission, your Majesty,' said Llewellyn to King John, 'I should like my wizard to show the company what he can do.'

When the King, the princes, the nobles and the magnificently dressed English wizard saw this poor-looking ragged man, they laughed ; but the King gave his permission all the same, out of politeness to his guest.

Nervously Llewellyn whispered to the red-haired one :

'I hope that you are indeed as clever as you make out for I have little wish to be shamed in front of these English lords.'

'Have no fear,' said the red-haired wizard and, without more ado, he snapped his fingers and the sea again seemed to come into the banqueting hall, but this sea was of an incredible colour, neither blue nor green, but a mixture of both, and the ships that sailed on it were of silver and gold, their prows encrusted with precious jewels, and their merchandise of silks, spices and exotic fruits piled high in their bows for all to see.

Snapping his fingers again, the wizard made the sea and ships disappear, and in the middle of the hall a great oak appeared, its leafy branches throwing shadows over the dining tables, and its acorns falling to the floor where a herd of pigs appeared to eat

139

them. Then twenty-four servants were conjured out of the air who began to chase away the pigs.

The King's wizard had watched this show of magic with a jealous heart, and now he said :

' This is but Welsh trickery, and not true magic at all.'

Whereupon the red-haired man touched him with his wand and he turned into a buck. The twenty-four servants turned into twenty-four hounds who, leaping at the buck, instantly killed him.

The company were too amazed and startled to say anything, but Llewellyn said :

' You are a great wizard indeed.'

Then the King spoke :

' We are deeply impressed by this exhibition ; little did we think to see such wonders. I could wish though that my own wizard had not been taken from me in this fashion.'

The red-haired wizard bowed low to the King, then he struck the body of the dead buck with his wand, and it turned back into the old man, alive and well, and none the worse for his adventure.

Llewellyn left the court in a blaze of glory, and was about to return to his humble lodgings in another part of London when the red-haired man stopped him, saying :

' My lord, your dwelling-place is not fit for a prince of Wales. Look, here is a palace for you.'

And with a wave of his wand, he produced a wonderful palace right in front of them. And the Prince dwelt there in happiness and comfort for three months and a fortnight.

When the time came for Llewellyn to return to Wales, his palace was well known and admired, and many wealthy men tried to rent it from him, offering him enormous sums of money for it.

PRINCE LLEWELLYN AND THE RED-HAIRED MAN

But the man of the red hair said :

' Do not accept their offers for I must take this palace away.'

So Llewellyn refused every offer for it and, on the day of departure, the wizard drew his wand along the walls, and the palace was no longer there.

Back to Wales rode Llewellyn, his men and the red-haired wizard, until they came to the place Cefn Tegeingl, near Trefriw, where they had first met the ragged man.

' I must leave you now,' he said to Llewellyn, ' but I should like you to know that I am an angel sent to help you by Mary of Trefriw and to save you from shame at the court of King John. Continue to pray to St Mary, and she will guide and guard you.'

That was the last Prince Llewellyn saw of his red-haired friend, but he never forgot him, and he remained devoted to St Mary of Trefriw for the rest of his life.

Fairy Ointment ≈◦

PALI was preparing supper in her kitchen when the fairy called
on her. Now Pali was a famous midwife in the county where
she lived, and had helped many babies to come into the world,
so she was not surprised when the fairy at the door said to her :
'Pali, Pali, come quickly with me, my fairy mistress needs
your help with her baby.'

Pali put on her cloak and bonnet and took her supper of stew
off the fire ; she hoped she would get something to eat wherever
it was she was going, for she was very hungry. Then she locked
her cottage door and, without more ado, clambered on to a
handsome horse behind the fairy who was already astride it ;
and they rode off into the dark.

The horse was very fleet of foot ; Pali felt she was riding
through the air rather than over the stony ground, and the
horse's back was so comfortable she might still have been sitting
in her rocking-chair in the kitchen.

'Who is your mistress, and where does she live ?' asked Pali
of her fairy companion.

'She is the wife of one of our princes, a much-loved woman,
and she lives in the country we shall soon have reached,' replied
the fairy, adding, 'I hope you are prepared to stay a few days.'

Pali nodded her head ; a visit to the fairies would make a nice
change, and what a wonderful story she would have to tell her
friends and neighbours on her return !

FAIRY OINTMENT

In no time at all the horse came to rest in front of what seemed to be a very grand palace, although it was too dark for Pali to see it clearly. She followed the fairy through a magnificent doorway, and into a blaze of light that revealed a hall of space and splendour, off which led a number of equally splendid rooms. In one of these, on a beautifully carved bed covered with sheets of pale green silk and blankets of white swansdown, lay the fairy princess.

She welcomed Pali warmly, and it was not long before the baby was born. The midwife was given instructions to look after the baby well, to wash it carefully and to dress it warmly.

' Oh, and Pali,' added the mother, ' here is some ointment with which you must rub my baby night and morning after you have washed him, but do not touch it yourself except with your hand and, above all, never put it to your eyes,' and she handed Pali a little box with a lid of mother-of-pearl and full of a soft pink cream.

The days went by, and Pali lived in comfort. Everything she needed was given her and she was well cared for and well fed, but the strange thing was that, although the things she needed always appeared at the right time, and food and drink were served on the dining-table, Pali never saw or heard the people who did these jobs. In fact she saw only the fairy princess and her baby.

One day when Pali had finished anointing and dressing the baby, one of her eyes began to itch and, forgetting the Princess's instructions, she rubbed it with her hand on which some of the ointment still remained. Immediately she saw the palace was full of all sorts of lovely things she had never noticed before. The beauty of the flowers, the tapestries, the furniture and the china was almost overwhelming. She said nothing about this, but as the day wore on she noticed more and more, and even began to see small men and women going about their daily jobs. They moved as softly and as lightly as a summer breeze, and as quickly as the hares that Pali sometimes disturbed outside her cottage. They prepared the food with daintiness and skill, and waited on their fairy mistress with tender care and affection.

Other little men and women came and went during the course of the day, most of them staying for an hour or so to chat with the Princess and to see the new baby. But by evening they had all left, and Pali was getting the baby ready for bed when she chanced to say to the Princess :

'I hope you are not too tired, my lady, for you have had a great many visitors today.'

The Princess raised her dark eyebrows in surprise and demanded :

'How do you know that, Pali ?'

Pali was at once put in confusion, and blushed and murmured her apologies.

'You have been putting ointment to your eyes,' accused the fairy princess. 'Well, Pali, now you must go home for you have seen more than any human should in this place. Thank you for your services, all the same ; you shall be well rewarded for your care of my child.'

And indeed when the same fairy who had brought her to the palace left her at her cottage door, Pali found that she had in her hands a bag of gold coins. She also had, unknown to the fairy, the half-full jar of fairy ointment.

It soon became known in the district that the midwife had magic powers, and that she could see fairy folk who were invisible to the ordinary human eye.

But Pali did not possess her magic powers for long. One morning she went to the fair at a nearby town, and there she saw a group of fairies doing business in the market square. To her delight, she noticed in the middle of them the lovely fairy princess whose baby she had looked after and who had always been so sweet and kind to her. Rushing up to her, Pali warmly greeted the fairy lady.

' Good morning, madam, what a pleasure it is to see you here, and looking so well, too.'

The Princess turned and angrily faced Pali.

' You have no right to be seeing me here at all,' she hissed and then she spat into Pali's eyes.

At that moment the fairy lady and her fairy friends vanished completely in front of Pali's eyes, and never again was she able to see any one of the fairy race.

Cadwalader and his Goat 🐐

CADWALADER owned a beautiful black-and-white nanny-goat, and this goat's name was Jenny. Jenny was a good goat, and she was fond of her master and he of her. She never caused him any trouble, and he repaid her by feeding her well and seeing that she was kept warm in the winter.

Because she had always been such a docile animal, Cadwalader was surprised when, one day, she behaved rather badly. Instead of staying happily in the field where her master was working and where she usually spent her time nibbling at the sweet grass under the hedges, Jenny suddenly leapt over the hedge and galloped away. Startled by the clatter of her hooves as she jumped, Cadwalader looked up from his work, and began to race after his precious goat. He certainly didn't want to lose her.

'And what has got into her anyway?' he asked himself. 'Why is she behaving in this fashion?'

He, too, leapt over the hedge, and there he saw Jenny scampering over the next field. After her went Cadwalader, over the next field and the next, and then up the steep and rocky path that led to the mountains. Here, of course, Jenny had a great advantage, for goats are sure-footed and well used to climbing in difficult places; but poor Cadwalader slowed down and sometimes fell down, but he always managed to pick himself up and never quite lost sight of Jenny.

He had never lost his temper with her before, but he was

146

The goats set up a terrible bleating

tired with the chase and picked up a small rock and threw it at the goat. His aim was good, the rock hit her on the side and with such force that she toppled over a precipice that lay to the right of her.

Cadwalader was filled with remorse for what he had done, and he climbed down quickly to where Jenny lay, still breathing faintly. He crouched down beside her and, lifting her head, Jenny just managed to put out her tongue and lick his hand. Overcome by what seemed to him a gesture of forgiveness on the goat's part, Cadwalader burst into tears. He took Jenny's head on his lap and tried to comfort the dying animal, whispering to her softly and gently smoothing the rough hair.

Time went on, and the moon rose. The hair beneath Cadwalader's fingers seemed softer and silkier. He peered into Jenny's face and found he held in his arms not a goat at all, but a beautiful young maiden with long brown hair and huge brown eyes that gazed fondly into his.

'Ah, Cadwalader,' sighed the goat maiden, 'have I at last found you?'

Rising to her feet, the maiden took Cadwalader's hand and

led him up and over the mountains. Cadwalader was enchanted with the lovely maiden and pressed her hand in his as they walked along together ; but he could not help thinking as he did so that her hand felt remarkably like a hoof.

Presently they came to the top of a high mountain and found themselves in the middle of a flock of goats, whose shadowy forms looked huge in the moonlight. As soon as Cadwalader and his companion began to move among them, the goats set up a terrible bleating that echoed over the mountains and into the valleys below. Cadwalader felt that he was not at all welcome here, although the maiden was obviously quite at home.

One of the goats, bigger than the rest and making as much noise on his own as the others put together, was apparently their king. He looked at Cadwalader in such an unfriendly fashion that the young man loosed the maiden's hand and began to back away. Then the goat king lowered his head and, with a tremendous bellow, charged at poor Cadwalader, butting him in the stomach and knocking him over a crag as, earlier in the evening, Cadwalader had done to his own Jenny.

The young man lay there unconscious until the next morning when the warm sunshine seeped into his bruised flesh and bones, and the song of the early birds awakened him from his stupor.

He crawled home with faint hope in his heart, but when he reached his fields there was no Jenny to greet him, and he never again saw her or the maiden she became for that short time.

Shakespeare must have heard about this story, for in his play, *Henry V*, Pistol refuses to eat the leek offered him by Fluellen, saying :

'No. Not for Cadwalader, and all his goats.'

St Cadog and the Mouse ≈●

ST CADOG and his disciples had been visiting Ireland and, on their return, came to Breconshire, where the saintly man wished to stay a while that he might improve his Latin. He hoped to do this with the help of a learned Italian who had settled in Wales.

When Cadog visited the Italian to ask if he might be his pupil, the foreigner hesitated a moment.

' What is the matter ? ' asked Cadog.

' Well, it's like this, sire,' explained the Italian : ' you and your disciples are welcome here, and I will gladly teach you all I can ; but there is a severe famine in the land, and I do not know how you are to be fed.'

' I shall pray to God for His help,' said Cadog simply, and he went away to his prayers.

Later that same day Cadog was writing at his desk when he heard a rustling among his papers. Looking up from his work, he noticed a little mouse scampering about on his desk. He was a happy little mouse and Cadog did not shoo him away but watched him a while, smiling at his antics. The mouse looked at Cadog, his whiskers twitching and his tiny eyes bright with mischief ; then he moved on to Cadog's writing paper, and on it he dropped from his mouth one piece of corn.

' Thank you, little mouse,' said Cadog gravely.

The mouse ran off, down the leg of the desk and to the

The mouse looked at Cadog

corner of the room, where he disappeared through a hole in the wall.

A few minutes later, the mouse returned, clambered on to the desk and dropped another grain in front of St Cadog, who again said :

' Thank you, little mouse.'

Seven times the mouse came and went, each time bringing with him one grain of corn until there was a little golden heap lying on Cadog's writing-paper.

' It is a sign from heaven ! ' exclaimed Cadog, and at once sent for his Italian friend.

' Can you find me a piece of thread ? ' he asked him.

' Yes, I have some in my pocket there,' was the reply, ' but what do you want it for ? '

' You'll see, you'll see,' Cadog told him and, catching the mouse gently in his hand, he proceeded to tie the end of a long fine thread of silk to the mouse's foot. Then he released the animal, which at once disappeared through its hole in the wall.

Cadog followed the mouse's trail by way of the silken thread until at last he arrived in a field where there was a heap of soil piled high like a small hill. The mouse had disappeared into this, and Cadog started to dig his way in with the help of the Italian.

When they had dug for some hours they came to the remains of a beautiful old house, and inside the house was a huge room full of good clean corn where the little mouse was nibbling away to his heart's content.

This store of corn not only provided the necessary food for Cadog and his disciples but it also helped to relieve the suffering of the starving people in the district. Later on, when the famine was over, St Cadog built a monastery on the spot where he had found the old house, as a memorial to God and a thanksgiving for the time when He sent one of His small creatures in answer to a humble prayer.

St Cadog and King Arthur 🖋

A BRITISH general called Ligessawc had killed three of Arthur's soldiers and, although he had done this in fair battle, King Arthur was angry with him and determined to take him prisoner.

The general fled from one part of the country to another, always hotly pursued by Arthur's men. No-one would shelter him because fear of Arthur was too great, but at last he crossed into Wales where he sought refuge with St Cadog. Here he was not refused, and he led a quiet life, praying in the monastery and helping Cadog and his monks in the fields for seven happy years. King Arthur had no idea where he was until finally someone betrayed him.

One day a messenger came to St Cadog, his clothes torn and his eyes full of terror.

' Master,' he cried, ' a great army of Arthur's men is camped on the other side of the river, and Arthur is demanding the surrender of Ligessawc.'

Hearing this, Ligessawc was prepared to give himself up rather than harm the good man and his monks who had befriended him.

' But,' said Cadog, ' nonsense, you asked for, and have received, refuge in God's house, and here you shall stay. This matter can surely be settled with words, and not with blows.'

ST CADOG AND KING ARTHUR

And he went down to the riverside alone. On the other side of the river, which was the river Usk, was the huge array of Arthur's army, their tents swaying in the breeze, their armour glittering in the sun and their war-horses for the moment peacefully cropping the smooth grass.

' I wish to speak with Arthur,' shouted Cadog over the water.

' He wants no speech,' came back the answer ; ' he wants Ligessawc.'

' Nonetheless I would have speech with Arthur,' repeated Cadog and, impressed with the brave lone figure of this monk, a messenger went to Arthur, and returned a short time later with the huge and handsome king.

' Is Ligessawc there, holy man ? ' shouted Arthur.

' Yes,' said Cadog, ' he is at my monastery.'

' Well, then, let's have an end to this. Surrender him to me or my army and I will come across and get him.'

' I'll not surrender him,' defied Cadog. ' He asked for refuge and he received it. Surely a man of your honour and courage will understand that I cannot be so cowardly as to hand him over because of your threats.'

Arthur was silent, recognising the fairness of these words.

' This is a matter for discussion,' continued Cadog. ' You are known to be a man of justice as well as a man of courage. Will you agree to submit this problem to chosen judges ? I will stand by their verdict if you will do the same.'

After much deliberation, Arthur agreed to this. Five famous judges were found, and each party took up its stand on its own side of the river.

Argument began and went on for many days. Arthur at last agreed to accept payment in kind instead of the person of Ligessawc.

'Three cows for each of Arthur's soldiers,' was suggested by someone on the Welsh side of the river.

'Not enough,' came back a roar from the English side.

At last the judges announced that, in their view, Arthur should be given a hundred cows for each of his soldiers.

It was now that Arthur began to prove difficult.

'I refuse to have cows of all one colour, mind you,' he said. 'They must be red in front and white at the back.'

There was consternation among Cadog's supporters when they heard this, and no amount of persuasion would make Arthur change his mind. The judges were of the opinion that, as Arthur had given up his claim to Ligessawc himself, he was entitled to make this extraordinary demand.

'Who has ever heard of cows that are red in front and white at the back?' asked a bewildered monk.

'And where are they to be found?' asked Ligessawc.

'Don't worry,' said Cadog, 'some of you men fetch me the required number of cows of any colour, and ask no further questions.'

The cows were duly found and herded together on the river bank. Cadog scarcely looked at them, but he raised his hand, murmured a few words, and the cows at once changed to red in the front and white at the back.

Arthur was furious when he saw what had happened; he had been sure that his demand could not be met, and had intended then to insist on Ligessawc's surrender.

There was yet another problem: how to get the cows to Arthur. The judges had further discussion, and directed Cadog's men to drive the herd half-way across the Usk and Arthur's men to be responsible for them from there on.

Cadog's men did as they were told and began to drive the

The huge and handsome king stood on the bank of the river

red-and-white cows into the water but, before they were half-way across, Arthur's men, in their haste to lay hands on their great prize, began to seize the animals and pull them to their own side by the horns. But, alas for their greed, as they did so, the prized possessions turned into bundles of hay in their hands.

Thus did the magic of the simple St Cadog triumph over the strength and might of the great King Arthur himself.

The House with the Front Door at the Back ⌇

A FARMER living at a place called Deunant was having trouble with his cattle. Never a very prosperous farmer, he was now in terrible difficulties because his herd was suffering from a disease called black-quarter, and was of little value to him. He came to the conclusion that the cattle had been bewitched by old Beti, whom it was rumoured in the village was some sort of witch. Certainly, she had called a few weeks earlier at his farm and begged to be given one of the geese which the farmer's wife was busy plucking.

'No, we can't spare one,' the farmer had told her, 'we have little enough for ourselves,' and the old woman had gone off, cursing.

So now the farmer paid her a visit to demand that she take her curse off his cattle. The old woman was crouching over the fire stirring a nasty-smelling brew when the farmer walked into her cottage.

'What can I do for you?' she muttered.

'I'll tie your hands and feet and throw you into the river if you don't take your evil curse off my cattle,' the farmer said angrily.

'I didn't curse your cattle,' whined old Beti. 'In spite of what they say about me in the village, I'm no witch.'

'Repeat the Lord's Prayer then and prove your innocence,' instructed the farmer.

Old Beti did this without a mistake, but still the farmer was not convinced.

' Say " God's blessing be on the cattle ",' he said. This was supposed to free bewitched cattle from disease.

' God's blessing be on the cattle,' repeated Beti promptly.

But the farmer's talk with old Beti had done no good ; his cattle remained diseased.

One night before going to bed, the farmer stood outside his front door to smoke a last pipe of tobacco, and to muse upon his problem.

' I really don't know what I have done to deserve such misfortune,' he said out aloud.

' Don't you ? ' said a squeaky little voice. ' I do.'

The farmer looked around him, and could see no-one there.

' I thought someone spoke,' he murmured.

' Someone did,' said the same squeaky little voice. ' I did. Look out, you clumsy wretch, you nearly stepped on me then.'

Looking down, the farmer saw at his feet a tiny man with a red feather in his hat and a very angry look on his face.

' I'm sorry,' said the farmer, ' but did I hear you say that you know why I am having trouble with my cattle ? '

' Certainly I know,' said the little man. ' Didn't I put the curse on them myself ? '

' But why ? ' asked the puzzled farmer. ' What have I ever done to you ? '

' You and your family are always annoying me and mine,' snapped the little man.

' In what way ? ' asked the farmer.

' Well, you are always throwing slops down the chimney of my house. Your front door opens, out your wife throws potato water, out your daughter throws whey after she's finished making cheese, out you throw your dirty washing-water. How would

157

you like all that mess coming down your chimney and flooding your house ? '

' I don't understand,' said the farmer. ' Naturally we throw the slops out here, we've no other door to throw them out of. But there's no house within miles of here ; how can they possibly go down anyone's chimney ? '

' Put your foot on mine,' the small man ordered, ' and you'll see that I'm speaking the truth.'

The farmer obeyed, gently placing his big foot on the tiny one of the small man, and there below him he could see what he had never seen before, a little street and in it a little house whose chimney, it was true, lay right in the way of where he and his family always threw their slops. As soon as he removed his foot from the little man's, he could no longer see street, house or chimney.

' Well, well, all I can say is that I'm very sorry indeed,' the farmer apologised and, being a kind and thoughtful man, he added, ' Is there anything at all I can do to make up for this annoyance ? '

The little man smiled for the first time.

' There is,' he said. ' You can remove the annoyance ; wall up this door and make another at the back of your house, then your slops will do me and my family no more harm.'

With that, he vanished completely, leaving the farmer unsure if he had been dreaming or awake. Still, he was willing to try anything that might result in the cure of his cattle, and he spent the next week blocking up his door and building another at the back. No sooner was this completed than his cattle recovered, and it was not long before the farmer became a prosperous man who never minded the jokes of his friends about the odd house in which he lived that had the front door at the back.

The Disappearance of Rhys

RHYS and Llewellyn were farm labourers; they worked together on the same farm and were great friends. They did not live on the farm where they worked, but in cottages in the village not far away.

One evening at dusk they were returning home from work when Rhys stopped suddenly and grabbed Llewellyn's arm.

'Can you hear anything?' he asked.

Llewellyn listened for a moment, then replied:

'Only the sighing of the wind and the last twittering of the birds.'

'Nothing else?'

'No, nothing. Why?' asked Llewellyn.

'Do you not hear faint sounds of music, such music that would set your feet a-dancing merrily all night?'

Llewellyn was tired and hungry and anxious to get home, and it was with impatience that he said:

'Really, Rhys, what nonsense you talk. I hear no music, and it's high time that you and I were home.'

But Rhys refused to move, and he strained his ears to catch further sound of the delightful music.

'I must stay and listen,' he said. 'You go on home. I'll catch you up,' and he turned his back on Llewellyn who walked on towards the village, not unduly worried about his friend but suspecting he wanted to go off for a drink somewhere, or to meet his girl.

Next morning Rhys still had not turned up, and Llewellyn had to go to work alone.

At the farm Rhys's relations had already been making inquiries about him ; and the farmer had told them he only knew that the labourer had left, as usual, the evening before in the company of his friend Llewellyn. And Llewellyn was himself unable to give them much further information.

' It seems to me,' said one of Rhys's brothers, ' that Llewellyn here could tell us more if he so wished.'

And when the countryside had been searched for the missing man and still he had not been found, suspicion did indeed fall upon Llewellyn, and it was murmured that, as Llewellyn had been the last to see Rhys, it looked as if he might have murdered him. In vain did the wretched Llewellyn protest his innocence, and he was put in prison to await his trial.

However, the farmer for whom Rhys and Llewellyn worked, refused to believe that Llewellyn was guilty. He knew the man to be a good worker and an honest fellow. He knew that Rhys and Llewellyn never quarrelled, and he could see no possible reason why Llewellyn should have wished to murder his best friend. Together with other good friends of the prisoner, he went to visit him in gaol.

' Llewellyn,' said the farmer, ' we have come to help you. I have thought a great deal about the conversation you last had with Rhys, and I have come to the conclusion that the music he heard was fairy music and that he has been kidnapped by the fairies. Possibly he strayed into a fairy ring.'

' Yes, I daresay,' agreed Llewellyn, ' but how is that going to help me ? '

THE DISAPPEARANCE OF RHYS

' We can get Rhys back from the fairies,' replied the farmer, ' and thus prove your innocence, but we must be quick about it. You have been many months in gaol, and it was many months before that when Rhys disappeared.'

' But why the hurry ? ' asked one of the other men.

' If we don't hurry I'll be hanged for his murder, that's why,' said Llewellyn.

' Not only that,' said the farmer, ' but we must rescue him a year and a day after his disappearance because that is as long as the fairies stay in any one place and, once they have moved off, Rhys may well be with them for ten, twenty or a hundred years, and we shall have no idea where to look for him.'

' What are we to do then ? ' asked Llewellyn.

The farmer told him that it would be necessary for Llewellyn to take them to the spot where he had last seen Rhys ; then he arranged for Llewellyn to be allowed out of gaol for a few hours.

The farmer and Llewellyn's friends wandered over the ground at the spot Llewellyn indicated, with no result whatsoever, until Llewellyn himself cried out :

' Hush, hush, I can hear the music of harps.'

The farmer bade Llewellyn stay exactly where he was for he had one foot just inside a fairy ring.

' Put your foot on Llewellyn's,' he told one of the friends, ' and see if you can hear the music too.'

The friend gingerly placed his foot on Llewellyn's, and a smile at once crossed his lips.

' Yes, yes, I hear music, wonderful music,' he said.

One by one the friends placed a foot on Llewellyn's and, in turn, each heard the fairy music. And at last they also saw the little people. There seemed hundreds of them, and they were hopping, prancing, capering and dancing round and round until the very sight of them made the onlookers dizzy.

'Look, look,' called out Llewellyn, 'there is Rhys himself, dancing like a madman !'

Sure enough, there was Rhys, whirling round with the little people as if he had not a care in the world.

'Grab him when next he comes round,' advised the wise farmer.

Llewellyn waited his chance, and when Rhys danced towards him, he seized him and, using all his strength, pulled him out of the ring.

Rhys appeared dazed, and obviously had no idea how long he had been dancing. On the day of his disappearance he and Llewellyn had been sent by the farmer to look for some lost horses in the hills, and Rhys's first words now were :

'Where are the horses ? Where are the horses ? '

'Found a year ago, you idiot ! ' said Llewellyn.

Delighted to have found the lost man, the company set off home in high spirits, but Rhys did not seem quite as pleased. They had not gone far when he announced his intention of returning to the fairy ring.

'To be sure,' said he wistfully, 'that music and dancing were most jolly. I think I'll go back for more. I was hardly there any time.'

But Llewellyn had suffered enough from his friend's absence and shook him hard by the arm as if to shake some sense into him.

'Look, Rhys,' he said, 'this has been a serious business. You've been there long enough to come near getting me hanged, and I'll have no more of it.'

When the full story was told him, Rhys agreed to stay with

his friends, but oftentimes when he and Llewellyn were working in the fields he would stop for a moment, raise his head and strain to hear the lovely music that had once enchanted him, and only a fierce pinch from Llewellyn would bring him back to earth and to work !

Shon Shenkin ✺

ONE fine summer morning a young man called Shon Shenkin
was on his way to work in the fields. He loitered a little to
watch the rabbits at play, and to pick a few wild flowers from the
hedgerows ; but it was the bird-song that really delayed him for
it was especially lovely that morning. Shon was very familiar
with the songs of the birds and could easily tell the thrush from
the blackbird ; in fact he knew all the different species of birds in
his district by sight as well as sound. That is why, on this particular morning, he was surprised to hear an unfamiliar note among
the rest. He traced it to a little bird in a nearby sycamore tree.

Quietly Shon made his way to the tree, sat himself beneath
its shady branches and listened to the little bird singing. And,
oh, how sweet and enchanting was its song ! Shon felt he could
have stayed there for ever listening to this magical music, but
there was work to do in the fields and, when at last the bird
stopped singing, Shon roused himself and got up. It was with
astonishment that he now looked at the tree under which he had
been sitting. Surely it had only been a slender young tree that
had sheltered him, yet this was a huge old tree with decayed
trunk and dead branches. Shon rubbed his eyes but the huge
tree was still there, and he told himself he must have imagined
the young sycamore.

He went on to the fields but, when he reached them, he found
the other men had finished work and gone home for their dinner.

How sweet and enchanting was the bird's song !

' Good gracious ! ' exclaimed Shon, ' I have wasted a lot of time this morning,' and he turned round and made for his own home and his own dinner, telling himself that he would work doubly hard that afternoon to make up for the time he had lost that morning.

Shon Shenkin walked quickly up the path to the little house where he lived with his mother and father. He noticed that the flower beds had been newly tended ; there were different plants growing there from the ones he had seen when he set out a few hours earlier. Unlike he, how busy his mother must have been that morning ! Shon opened the door and, as he walked into the house, he nearly knocked down an old man he had never seen before.

' Look where you're going,' muttered the old man.

' And what are you doing here anyway ? ' asked Shon.

' What am I doing here ? What am I doing here ? ' cried out

the old man. ' What a question to ask ! Who do you think you are, insulting a poor old man in his own house ? '

' *Your* house ? ' asked Shon. ' I'm afraid I don't understand. You are a stranger to me, and this is my house. Where are my mother and father ? '

The old man sensed that something was wrong and took the young man into the parlour, where Shon told him about the enchanting singing of the bird and the strange tree that was young one moment and old the next.

' I remember,' said the old man, ' how my grandfather used to tell me that his uncle went out one morning and was never seen again. Is your name Shon Shenkin ? '

Shon weakly nodded his head.

' A wise old woman said you were under the spell of the fairies,' continued the old man, ' and that you would not be released until the sap of the sycamore tree would be dried up. Come here, Shon, and embrace your great-great-grand-nephew.'

But as the two men embraced, poor Shon, who was really such an old old man, crumbled into a handful of dust.

The Little Red Bogie-Man ✒

GLYN was a farmer's son who worked on his father's farm ; but the farmer had other sons whom he favoured, and Glyn was not happy at home. He was given the hardest work to do and the least praise for doing it, and he was treated more like a servant than a son of the house.

One day he decided to run away from home and seek his fortune elsewhere so, first taking the few coins he had managed to save from under the mattress of his bed where he had hidden them, he then cut himself a stout stick of ash and set off. He didn't know where he was going or what he was going to do, but he was a lad of courage and high spirits, and he was sure that he would meet with good luck. Even a couple of encounters with highwaymen, when his ash stick proved useful in his defence, did not daunt him.

Weeks went by, and Glyn wandered from village to village, now and again helping a farmer on the land in return for food and shelter, and sometimes taking on other odd jobs at the village smithy, mill or bakehouse. Wherever he went he met with kindness, and he was never refused a bed for the night.

But one night he found himself in a strange part of the country with not a house in sight. He was tired and footsore and had almost decided to lie down under a hedge, in spite of the heavy rain that was falling, when he saw a faint light in the far distance. He tramped on until at last he saw the outline of a solitary farmhouse. This spurred him on, and soon he was knocking at the farmhouse door. It was opened by a man with a friendly face and cheerful grin.

' And what can I do for you, my lad ? ' he asked.

' I wonder if I might have a night's lodging with you,' said Glyn. ' I have travelled far this day and am wet and weary.'

' You would be welcome here,' said the man of the house. ' I never refuse hospitality, but unfortunately we have a great number of guests and the house is full.'

Glyn's face fell ; he murmured that it didn't matter and he was about to turn round and go off into the rain, when the man put a hand on his arm.

' Don't go, lad,' he said. ' I hate the idea of you having nowhere to sleep on a night like this. I have a house in the woods over there that is always empty at night, although I'm not sure it would be suitable.'

' Anything with a roof over it will do, even if it leaks,' interrupted Glyn eagerly.

' Oh, it's water-tight enough,' assured the man, ' it's not that. And it's warm ; there's a nice fire there ; we use the place in the day.'

' You are afraid I might make it dirty,' said Glyn, gazing ruefully at his tattered, wet and muddy clothes.

' No, no, it's not that either. The truth is that neither I, my family nor my servants will sleep there because a spirit disturbs the place. And I don't much like the thought of you sleeping there either ; it might not be safe.'

' Is that all ! ' laughed Glyn. ' Why, I can assure you I shall be pleased to stay there, with your permission. I'm not afraid of spirits ; I'm sure I shan't be harmed for indeed, as far as I know, I never harmed anyone myself in my life.'

THE LITTLE RED BOGIE-MAN

The man was still doubtful about the wisdom of Glyn spending the night in a haunted house, but Glyn continued to assure him that he did not share these fears, so he was given a basket of food and directed towards the woods.

Glyn walked quickly through the woods, where the rain from the trees dripped down inside his jacket and made him wetter than ever, until he came to the house, which looked a pleasant enough place although it was in a lonely spot.

Inside, everything was clean and tidy; and in the living-room there burned a huge and comforting fire. Glyn dried himself in front of this, and then sat down to eat the supper his kind host had provided. How he enjoyed the rich cold ham, the fresh bread, the home-made cheese and the big jug of milk! When he had finished he lay back in a chair, toasting his feet at the fire, and congratulating himself on his good fortune. The silence soothed him; he felt more contented than he had done for a long time. But what was that? Something had disturbed his thoughts, some sort of noise.

'Surely it is only a branch of a tree knocking against the window pane,' Glyn said aloud, and the sound of his voice echoed through the empty house. He relaxed again in the chair. But there it was again, louder, and now Glyn knew it did not come from outside the house; the knocking was too near. He listened carefully. The knocking was very near. It came from the chimney.

Then a voice spoke from the same place, and it grew louder and louder and louder.

'I am coming down,' it said. 'I am coming down. I am coming down.'

Glyn was not frightened, but he was cross that his peace had been disturbed; he went over to the chimney and called out:

' Come down then, and be hanged to you ! '

And down from the chimney there landed in the hearth a little man no more than three feet high who was red from head to foot—his clothes, his flesh, his hair, even his eyes. He was an alarming sight, but still Glyn was not frightened.

' Was it necessary to make all that noise ? ' he asked. ' You are not very big.'

At this the little red man hopped up and down in rage.

' Well, if I am small,' he screamed, ' here are two bigger than I,' and with that the door opened and in came two huge men carrying a coffin, which they placed on two chairs.

' Now you go outside until I call you,' ordered the little man, and the two huge men silently went off. ' And as for you '—the little red bogie-man turned to Glyn—' you come with me.'

' Look here,' said Glyn, ' I came here for some peace and quiet. Why don't you leave me alone ? No, I won't come with you.'

' Come with me,' repeated the little man furiously.

' Well,' replied Glyn, ' I don't want you to think I am afraid of you—I certainly am not—and to prove it to you, all right, I will come with you.'

The little man skipped out of the room and Glyn followed him, although he had some difficulty in keeping up with him. Up steps, down steps, along corridors, in and out of all sorts of rooms they went till at last they came to a flight of stone steps that led down into a cellar. At the top of these the little red man stepped aside and, pointing down below, he commanded :

' Go down.'

' No, I won't,' answered Glyn, who was beginning to be annoyed at the way this tiny man was ordering him about. ' Go down yourself.'

The command was repeated and so was Glyn's reply.

THE LITTLE RED BOGIE-MAN

' No, I won't.'

' For the last time,' said the little man, ' I order you to go down.'

' Oh, well,' agreed Glyn, ' I suppose I might as well agree in case you should think I am afraid of you,' and down the steps he went, followed by the little red bogie-man.

When they reached the bottom, the little man said in a more friendly tone.

' It's just as well that you obeyed, you know. If you hadn't, your body would soon have found its way to that coffin upstairs, and that would have been the end of you. Here, lift this stone.'

He pointed to a slab in the middle of the cellar floor, and this time Glyn did not stop to argue. He heaved at the slab until he managed to raise it, and underneath was a chest of gold.

' My goodness ! ' exclaimed the young man.

' I have waited for you for years,' said the little man, ' to put right a great wrong I once did. You didn't know it, but it was I who put it into your head to leave home, and it was I who directed your steps to this place. The gold must be divided with the good man who gave you permission to stay here, and he is to give you this house and the farmland surrounding it. You can then live here happily for the rest of your life. But see that neither of you acts unfairly, or the body of the one who does so will be in that coffin you saw, and he will not be seen again. I'll come back tomorrow night to make sure this gold has been evenly divided.'

Then he added crossly, as Glyn was too astonished to say anything :

' Woe betide you if it hasn't. And now, don't look round.'

With these words, he vanished, and Glyn, leaving the gold

where it was, found a comfortable bed in one of the many rooms in the house and soon fell fast asleep.

At daybreak the owner, who had been very anxious about the young man, arrived at the house with some of his servants. They knocked at the door. Glyn was too fast asleep to hear them. Again they knocked, and again there was no reply.

' Break the door in,' shouted the man to his servants. ' The spirit must have killed my young guest.'

The noise of the axes splintering the oak of the heavy front door at last woke Glyn, and he hurried down to see what was happening. The older man greeted him with relief and, when he had heard about the previous night's strange happenings, he quickly agreed to do what the little red man had suggested.

He and Glyn proved loyal friends and good partners. Neither he nor Glyn ever behaved unfairly, and so the coffin remained empty. In time the young man married one of the older man's lovely daughters, and they lived happily in the once haunted house.

The Bwgan Coch Bach, which is the Welsh for Little Red Bogie-Man, was never seen nor heard of again.

The Devil's Bridge 〜

THERE is in Wales a famous beauty spot called Devil's Bridge
—not a very nice name for such a pretty place—and this is the
story of how it came to be named.

In olden times it was a lonely place, a wild ravine where
the waters of the river roared and tumbled in a series of
waterfalls and collected in one spot to seethe and hiss in a
cauldron of nature's making that has since been called the Devil's
Punchbowl.

Old Megan lived near this ravine and, although she was poor
and only had one cow, she was happy enough until the day came
when she lost her cow. And what a stormy day that was ! The
wind howled and screamed in the trees, and the turbulent waters
of the river raced and bubbled faster than ever. Poor Megan
wrapped a shawl round her shoulders, put a hat on her head and
went off into the storm to search for her cow.

Her search led her to the ravine itself where, to her delight,
she espied the naughty cow, but her delight soon changed to
woe when she realised exactly where the cow was. How she
had got there Megan could not imagine. She was on the opposite
side of the river, placidly cropping the green grass, as if all were
right with the world.

' Oh, you bad creature ! ' shrieked Megan from her side of
the river, ' how am I going to get you back ? Was there ever
such a stupid animal as you ! '

The cow looked up for a moment on hearing Megan's familiar voice and gazed across the river at her, her velvet brown eyes soft and gentle as ever ; then she contentedly returned to her tasty meal.

'Oh, my goodness, what shall I do, what shall I do ? ' moaned old Megan, wringing her hands.

'What is the matter, old woman ? ' said a voice behind her which made Megan jump ; it was seldom that she met any other people in this lonely place. She turned round and saw a man, dressed like a monk, standing a few feet away from her. She hadn't heard him come but, there, the water was making so much noise and she had been shouting at the cow, so the sound of his footsteps might have been drowned anyway.

The stranger repeated his question and Megan, pointing across the river, explained what had happened.

'That cow is the only one I have. I am ruined if I can't get her back.'

The stranger came nearer, and patted her on the shoulder.

'Don't worry,' he said, 'I'll get her back for you.'

'How do you think you can do that ? ' asked Megan.

'Well, if there were a bridge across the river it would be simple, wouldn't it ? ' said the stranger.

'Of course it would,' snapped Megan, 'but it would take months to build and an army of men to build it, and it's hardly likely anyone is going to take all that trouble just to rescue poor old Megan's cow.'

'I could do it in a few moments, and on my own,' said the stranger. 'I have certain magic powers.'

'That's all very well,' answered Megan, 'but I'm a poor woman ; how should I repay you for such a service ? '

She turned round and saw a man dressed like a monk

'Just let me have the first living thing that crosses the bridge when it is built,' said the stranger, 'and I shall consider myself amply rewarded.'

Megan agreed to this apparently simple request, and the man told her to return to her cottage for a short time until he called her back. Megan reluctantly went home; she would dearly have liked to watch the stranger at his magic work.

On her way she began to do a little thinking, for old Megan was no fool. She had noticed something odd about the stranger: one of his feet had shown under his gown and it had looked like a hoof; also she had an idea that his knees were behind instead of in front.

'Just let me have the first living thing that crosses the bridge,' the man had said. Megan began to have her suspicions, and set about thinking of a way to cheat him.

By the time she heard his voice calling her back to the ravine, she had hit upon a plan. She had a little black dog and, telling him to follow her, she took a loaf of bread which she hid under her cloak, and off she went back to the riverside.

Well, the stranger had certainly kept his word. Spanning the river was a high and splendid bridge of fine proportions.

'There's your bridge for you,' announced the stranger proudly, 'and a pretty good one it is too.'

'Yes, perhaps it is and perhaps it isn't,' said Megan.

'What do you mean, perhaps it is and perhaps it isn't?' asked the stranger indignantly.

'Well, it's certainly a bridge and it *looks* very fine, but is it strong?' asked Megan.

'Of course it's strong!' exclaimed the man.

'Will it hold the weight of this, then?' asked the old woman, producing the loaf from under her cloak.

The stranger laughed. 'Hold the weight of that! Of course it will. Throw it on and see.'

Old Megan bowled the loaf across the bridge, and at the same time whistled to her little dog, who merrily scampered after it.

'Yes, it's strong enough,' she said; 'it holds the weight of the loaf and my little black dog. And by the way, kind sir, he is the first living thing to cross the bridge. I'll keep my bargain with you; you're welcome to him, and thanks very much for your trouble.'

176

At this the stranger stamped his foot with fury.

'The dog's no use to me,' he shouted and at once disappeared, leaving behind him a wisp of smoke and a smell of burning.

It was as wise old Megan had suspected. The stranger was the Devil himself, and he had hoped in his cunning to have possessed the old woman; but she was too clever for him and, as she crossed the Devil's Bridge to fetch her cow, she congratulated herself on gaining such a fine bridge and losing absolutely nothing.

The Changelings ✌️

A COTTAGER and his wife Gwyneth had long prayed that they should be blessed with a child, so you can imagine their great delight when Gwyneth gave birth not only to one child but to two ; and these twins, both boys, were fine, healthy, happy babies. How proud of them their father was, and how loving their mother ! He worked hard on his bit of land to provide food for them, and she nursed and looked after them with care and tenderness.

When the little boys were a few months old, one afternoon while their father was working in the fields, Gwyneth found she had no milk for them.

' Oh, dear,' she said to herself, ' I shall have to borrow some from our neighbours or the twins will cry all night with hunger.'

She put on her bonnet and shawl, kissed her babies goodbye, and told them she would not be gone for more than a few minutes. They lay in their cot, quite contented, and watched their mother go off down the path. Gwyneth didn't like leaving them alone, and she began to run that she would be back with them all the sooner. It was beginning now to get dark for it was late on a winter's afternoon. However, it was not long before she reached the neighbouring farm where she was given a big jug full of creamy milk.

' Have you left your babies all alone ? ' asked the farmer's wife.

THE CHANGELINGS

' Yes, I fear I have ; my husband, you see, is working in the fields,' replied Gwyneth, ' and the children must have milk. But I ran all the way here and shall run all the way back. They will not have been alone for more than a few minutes.'

' Well, hurry now,' advised her neighbour, ' it is beginning to get very dark.'

Gwyneth picked up her skirts and, running as best she could without spilling the milk, she made for home. On the way there she began to feel frightened. Bad fairies were known to live in the woods and fields, and this perhaps was why her neighbour had urged her to hurry home.

As she neared her cottage she noticed some shadowy shapes lurking against the blackthorn hedges. Poor Gwyneth was terrified ; as she neared the figures she recognised them as goblins, their funny ugly faces just visible underneath their untidy, uncombed hair. Not caring now if she did spill the milk, Gwyneth ran faster then ever, past the goblins, neither looking to the left nor to the right until she safely reached her own welcoming front door. She scarcely dared open the door. Supposing the bad fairies had stolen her babies : they were known to be terrible thieves ? Oh, what would she do if, when she opened the door, the cradle that only a few minutes ago had held her two bonny sons, now lay there empty ? She pushed open the door suddenly and, with relief and happiness, she saw the two babies lying asleep in their warm cradle.

When her husband returned from the fields Gwyneth smilingly told him what had happened and what foolish fears she had had after seeing the goblins.

' I'm quite certain they were goblins,' she told him, ' they were so ugly and evil looking. Still, they have done us no harm so I shall say no more about them.'

The weeks went by, and the twins seemed to make no progress. They grew no bigger although they ate their food, and they began to be cross and naughty, crying in the night for no good reason. Certainly they were quite unlike the healthy, happy babies they had once been. Their father was worried about them.

'There is something wrong with them, Gwyneth,' he said.

'Nonsense,' replied his wife, 'they are quite all right. They are not ill, and babies cannot be good and flourishing all the time. How like a man to think they should be fat and happy every day of the week, every week of the month, and every month of the year.'

'No, it is more than that,' said her husband, 'they do not somehow look like our babies used to look.'

'What do you mean?' demanded Gwyneth.

'Well, if you really want to know what I mean, I don't believe these are our children. I believe that on the day you went to borrow milk, the fairies stole our twins and left these in their place. At any rate, it is since that moment that the babies have changed so much for the worse.'

His wife refused to listen to him and, for the first time in their married life, they had a terrible squabble. Gwyneth's husband strode off to the fields, for it was harvest time, without even kissing her goodbye. After he had gone Gwyneth began to think about what he had said. She crossed to the cradle and looked closely at the babies. Their faces had altered, they looked bad-tempered and much uglier than they had once done. Was her husband right after all? She could not be sure, and decided to get advice on this difficult and worrying problem.

She went to see a very old and very wise man who lived alone in a cave and was always willing to help anyone in trouble. She told him her story and, when she had finished it, the old man was silent for five long minutes. Then he spoke.

'I cannot be sure, Gwyneth fach, from what you have told me, if the babies lying in the cradle at this moment are your own children or changelings.'

'Changelings?' asked Gwyneth.

'Changelings are the children the goblins leave in the place of the human babies they are so fond of stealing,' said the old man.

On hearing this, Gwyneth began to cry.

'Oh, dear,' she wailed, 'how am I going to find out if they are changelings, and what am I going to do?'

'Dry your eyes,' said the old man; 'I can tell you how to find out if they are changelings, and I can also tell you what to do when you have found out. Listen to me carefully. Tomorrow when you prepare dinner for the reapers, empty the shell of a hen's egg, fill the shell with stew, and take it out through the door as if you meant it for dinner for the reapers. If the babies are changelings, they will be surprised to see you do this, and they will speak. If they say nothing, they are your own children.'

The old man then told Gwyneth what to do if she discovered the children were changelings, and, greatly comforted, Gwyneth went home.

Next morning she began to follow the old man's directions. She took a brown egg, emptied out the egg from the shell and began to fill the shell with stew from a big pot she had boiling on the fire. She did this in front of the twins who watched her every movement. Then she went to the door with the egg shell in one hand and, opening the door, she called out:

'Reapers, reapers, come and get your dinner.'

No sooner had she spoken than, to her astonishment, she heard one of the twins say to the other:

' *Acorns before oak I knew,*
An egg before a hen,
Never one hen's egg-shell stew
Enough for harvest men ! '

Instantly Gwyneth, remembering the old man's words, realised these were not her own babies ; and she began to follow the rest of the wise man's directions. Snatching up the changelings from the cradle where they lay, she ran with them to a nearby pool. When she reached the pool she made as if to throw them in. In a second the wicked fairies had appeared to save their kin. There they stood, very angry to find themselves beaten ; and in the arms of one of them were Gwyneth's own children, as fat, as healthy and as happy as ever they had been. Another goblin snatched the fairy children from Gwyneth and put her own babies in her arms. Before Gwyneth could speak a word— although she would like to have told the bad fairies exactly what she thought of them—they and the changelings had completely disappeared.

Her husband was very pleased when Gwyneth returned with their own twins and told him what had happened. They never quarrelled again but, until the twins were old enough to look after themselves, Gwyneth never left them alone ; she could never be sure the goblins would not one day be up to their tricks again.

Printed by CSP Printing, Fairwater, Cardiff